Howard H. Gross

Teacher's Manual for the Andrews Lunar Tellurian

Howard H. Gross

Teacher's Manual for the Andrews Lunar Tellurian

ISBN/EAN: 9783337371548

Printed in Europe, USA, Canada, Australia, Japan

Cover: Foto ©Paul-Georg Meister /pixelio.de

More available books at **www.hansebooks.com**

TEACHER'S MANUAL

FOR THE

Andrews Lunar Tellurian

MANUFACTURED BY

A. H. ANDREWS & CO.

FIFTH EDITION.

A. H. ANDREWS & CO.,

195 Wabash Avenue, Chicago,   686 Broadway, New York.

1888.

Introduction.

TO THE TEACHER :

In the preparation of this Manual the writer has endeavored to treat the subjects presented, in a simple yet forcible manner, avoiding, as much as possible, technical terms. The illustrations given *outline* the work that should be done in the class-room. The teacher should, and no doubt will supplement these illustrations in many ways, presenting the subjects treated, step by step, in a thorough and yet attractive manner.

The value of *demonstration* is no longer doubted, and in those schools where it is most used the best results follow. This is pre-eminently true in geographical and astronomical work. The Lunar Tellurian is designed to furnish the illustrations necessary to give the pupils a comprehensive understanding of the relationships of the earth, sun and moon. It is so simple in construction that the average teacher may use it to advantage after a few hours' study with the Manual.

The teacher will find it advantageous to now and then assign a topic to one of the pupils, and require him to furnish clear and forcible demonstrations by use of the apparatus.

The teacher's attention is particularly called to the section in which Prof. E. Colbert, now scientific editor of the Chicago *Tribune*, and well known as a practical astronomer, treats the subject of Tides. His presentation is new, having reduced the *abstract* to the *concrete*. The author congratulates the readers upon being able to present an article from the pen of Prof. Colbert, and here acknowledges obligations to that estimable and scholarly gentleman.

The writer acknowledges his obligations to M. MacVicar, Ph. D., of the Michigan State Normal School—than whom there is no better authority on mathematical geography—some of whose illustrations the writer has embodied in this work.

Contents.

	PAGE.
...roduction,	3
...rews' Lunar Tellurian, Description,	5
How to Adjust the Lunar Tellurian,	6
Preparatory Work,	7
General Definitions,	8–16
Distribution of Light and Heat,	16–24
Days and Nights; Equal and Unequal,	24–27
The Sun's Apparent Path,	27–28
Change of Seasons,	28–30
Twilights,	30–33
The Sun's Declination,	34
To find the Latitude and Longitude of places,	35
Longitude and Time,	37–39
To find the Difference of Longitude between Two Places,	39–41
To find the Time of Sunrise and the Length of Twilight,	41
The Sun,	42–43
The Earth,	44–45
The Moon,	45–46
The Moon's Motions, Phases, etc.,	46–55
The Zodiac, Signs of, etc.,	55–59
Eclipses, Solar and Lunar,	59–68
Precession of the Equinoxes,	68–70
Equation of Time,	70–74
The Tides—*By Prof. Colbert*,	74–79
Solar System,	80–81

Andrews' Lunar Tellurian.

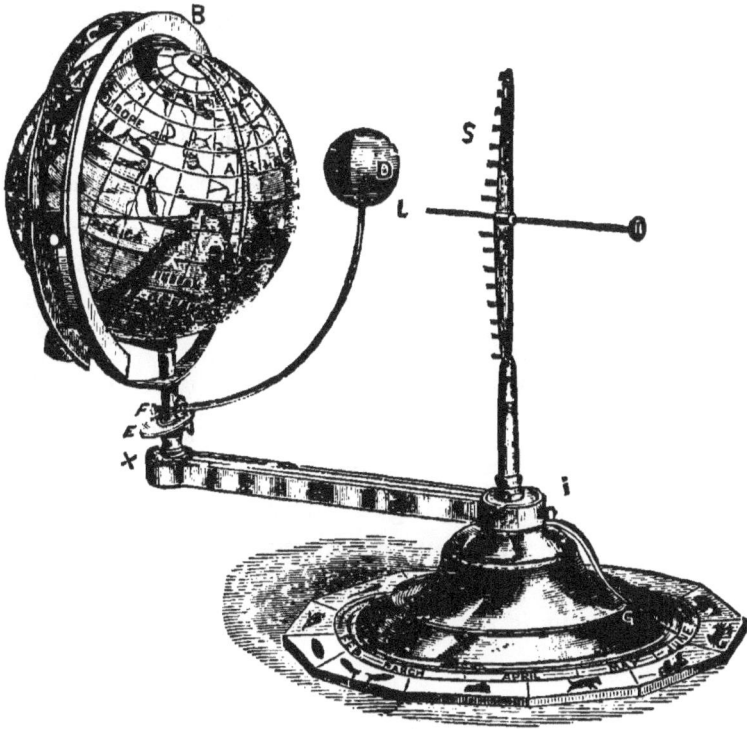

CUT NO. 1.

A is the Earth globe. S, an arc of the Sun's circumference; this arc extended to a circle would show the sun on the same scale as the earth globe. B, Circle of Illumination, or Day and Night Circle, showing how far sunlight extends. C, Twilight Circle, showing twilight limit. D, Moon ball, with light and dark hemispheres. F, gearing which keeps the moon's light hemisphere always toward the sun. E, plate showing inclination of moon's orbit. G, Calendar Index. L, pointer showing direction of the sun's central ray. H, Longitude or Time Index, for finding time of sunrise or sunset, length of day, night, and twilight. J, the Ecliptic. K, the Equator. I—X, the Main Arm of the Tellurian.

For lettering of other parts of the Lunar Tellurian see cut on page 36.

To Adjust the Lunar Tellurian.

To adjust the apparatus to agree with the calendar, move the arm IX until the calendar index G is opposite the 21st of June ; place the arm in which the south pole of the globe is fastened parallel with the arm IX, as shown in cut, or bring the calendar index to June 21st and place the center of the socket at the south pole opposite the mark I on the semi-circular brace joining the ends of circle C. The pointer L should be parallel with the arm IX.

Raise the moon ball until the gear wheels at F are *disengaged*, turn the cog·wheel to the right or left until the *white side* of the moon ball is toward the sun, drop the cogs into gear. The gearing will keep the bright side of the moon ball toward the arc S.

The apparatus is now fully adjusted for use.

For Geographical Study.

(The Globe may be used for geographical purposes and is an excellent one for such use, having the Isothermal Lines indicated in blue and red. The ocean currents are also shown. When thus used, the teacher will remove the circles B C, also the curved standards supporting the same (after lifting off the globe ball along with the axis.) Replace the globe, detach the moon also, at F, by tipping the ball toward the globe. The sun arc S, may also be removed. All these changes take but a moment, giving an unobstructed view of the Globe.)

Preparatory Work.

The study of the method of adjusting and handling the LUNAR TELLURIAN GLOBE in illustrating and solving problems.

Before using the globe in illustrations, the following points should be carefully studied. Each adjustment should be made familiar by actual practice. The teacher cannot be too particular on this point, as the power of any illustration depends largely upon the tact with which the piece of apparatus used is handled.

The cut on the preceding page represents the globe with all the attachments in position. Let every part be removed and replaced and set in the positions indicated again and again, until everything required can be done with ease and rapidity.

Be particular to notice the following suggestions :

1. The arc S represents the curvature of the surface of a ball which bears the same relation in size to the sun that the globe A bears to the earth. Hence by completing the circle of which the arc S is a part, and comparing it with a great circle on the globe, we have a correct representation of the relative size of the earth and sun.

2. The pointer L represents a line connecting the center of the earth and sun, hence, indicates the position of the only vertical ray of light or heat which comes from the sun to the earth.

3. The circle B is used to indicate the line which separates light from darkness ; hence is called the " Circle of Illumination," or " Day and Night Circle."

General Definitions.

The following definitions should be made familiar before commencing the use of the globe.

1. A **Point** is that which has position without magnitude.

2. A **Line** is the path of a moving point.

3. A **Straight Line** is one which has the same direction throughout its entire length.

4. A **Curved Line** is one which changes its direction at every point.

5. **Parallel Lines** are lines which have the same direction.

6. An **Angle** is the opening between two lines which meet in a common point called a *vertex*.

There are three kinds of angles, thus :

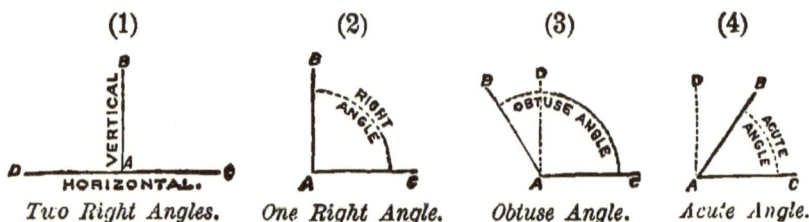

(1)	(2)	(3)	(4)
Two Right Angles.	*One Right Angle.*	*Obtuse Angle.*	*Acute Angle.*

7. When a line *meets* another line, making, as is shown (in 1), two *equal angles*, each angle is a **Right Angle,** and the lines are said to be perpendicular to each other.

8. An **Obtuse Angle** is an angle (as shown in **6**—3), that is *greater* than a *right angle.*

9. An **Acute Angle** is an angle (as shown in **6**—4), that is *less* than a *right angle.*

10. A **Plane** is a *surface* traced by a straight line moving in the same direction.

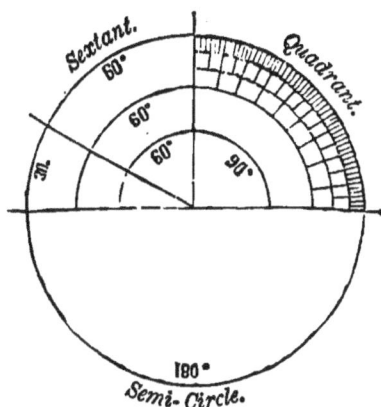

11. A **Circle** is a surface enclosed by a *curved line*, every point of which is *equally distant* from a point within called the *center*.

12. A **Circumference** is the line that bounds the circle.

In describing the lines on the surface of the globe, the word circle is used in place of circumference. When a *circle proper* is intended, the word "plane" is introduced.

13. A **Degree** is one of the 360 equal parts into which the *circumference* of a *circle* is supposed to be divided.

Observe, the length of a degree *varies* with the *size* of the circle.

14. The **Diameter** of a *circle* is a straight line passing through its center and *terminating* at *both ends* in the *circumference*.

15. The **Radius** of a *circle* is any straight line extending from its *center* to the *circumference*.

16. A **Sphere** is a solid or volume bounded by a curved surface, such that all points in it are equally distant from a point within called the center.

Observe the point *e.* in the cut in the margin, is the center of a sphere of which *c b d* is the lower half.

17. The **Diameter** of a *sphere* is a straight line passing through its center and terminating at both ends in the surface.

In the cut, *ab* and *cd* are *diameters*.

18. The **Radius** of a *sphere* is a straight line drawn from the center to any point in the surface.

In the cut, *ce, fe, ae, ge* and *de* are radii.

19. A **Great Circle** of a *sphere* is one whose plane passes through the center of the sphere.

Hence the planes of all great circles divide the sphere into two equal parts. Each part is called a Hemisphere.

20. A **Small Circle** of a *sphere* is one whose plane does not pass through the center of the sphere.

Hence, the planes of all small circles on a sphere divide the sphere into two unequal parts.

21. The **Axis** of the **Earth** is that diameter on which it rotates once in twenty-four hours.

22. The **Poles** of the **Earth** are the two points on its surface at the extremities of its axis.

23. The **North Pole** is the Pole *directed* to the North Star. The **South Pole** is the *opposite* extremity of the axis.

24. The **Equator** is a great circle midway between the poles whose plane is at right angles to the axis of the earth.

25. The **Parallels** of **Latitude** are small circles parallel to the Equator.

26. A **Meridian** is a semi-circle extending from Pole to Pole.

27. The **Latitude** of a place is its distance in degrees north or south of the Equator.

Places north of the Equator are said to be in *North Latitude*, and places south in *South Latitude*.

28. The **Longitude** of a place is its distance in degrees east or west of a given meridian called the *First* or *Prime* Meridian.

The meridian of the Royal Observatory at Greenwich, England, is commonly employed as the *Prime Meridian.* The French use the meridian of Paris ; the Germans that of Ferro, one of the Canary Islands ; and Americans frequently use that of Washington.

29. The **Tropic** of **Cancer** is a parallel of latitude 23½ degrees north of the Equator.

30. The **Tropic** of **Capricorn** is a parallel of latitude 23½ degrees south of the Equator.

31. The **Orbit** of the **Earth** is the path in which it moves round the sun.

Observe, the *plane* of the *earth's orbit* is the plane in which the orbit is described.

32. The **Zones** are broad belts or divisions of the earth's surface bounded by the Tropics and Polar Circles.

These four lines divide the surface of the earth into five zones or belts known as the *Torrid Zone*, the two *Temperate Zones*, and the two *Frigid Zones*.

The width of the Zones depends entirely upon the inclination of the axis. The width of the Torrid Zone is *double* the inclination of the axis (23½ degrees), or 47 degrees. The width of the Frigid Zone is *equal* to the inclination. The Temperate Zones embrace whatever surface lies between the Tropics and Polar Circles (43 degrees). If the inclination of the axis were 30 degrees, as in the case of the planet Saturn, the Zones would be as follows :

Torrid Zone, double the inclination,   30° or 60°
Frigid Zones, each equal to the inclination, 30° or 60°
Temp. Zones, each equal to the inclination, 30° or 60°

Total degrees from pole to pole,   -   -   180°

33. The **Ecliptic** is the sun's apparent yearly path through the fixed stars, or the *earth's* real path or *orbit*.

34. The **Zodiac** is a belt of the heavens 16 degrees wide, lying 8 degrees on each side of the Ecliptic, within which the sun, moon and planets are seen to move.

This belt is divided into twelve equal parts called *Signs of the Zodiac.* These divisions, with their names, are represented on the base of the Lunar Tellurian.

35. The **Equinoctial** or **Celestial Equator** is a *great circle* of the Celestial Sphere directly over the *terrestrial equator*, and hence is in the same plane.

36. The **Equinoctial Points** or **Equinoxes** are the points where the *Ecliptic* crosses the *Equinoctial.*

The point which the sun passes in March is called the *Vernal Equinox*, and that which he passes in September the *Autumnal Equinox.*

37 The **Solstitial Points** or **Solstices** are the two points where the sun is farthest from the Equinoctial.

The point north of the Equinoctial is called the *Summer Solstice*, and the one south the *Winter Solstice.*

38. The **Declination** of a heavenly body is its distance north or south from the Equinoctial.

Declination corresponds to terrestrial latitude.

39. Perihelion is the point in the earth's orbit nearest to the sun.

40. Aphelion is the point in the earth's orbit farthest from the sun.

41. Refraction in Astronomy is the change of direction which the rays of light undergo in passing through the atmosphere.

This may be illustrated to a class by placing on the blackboard a diagram ; thus,

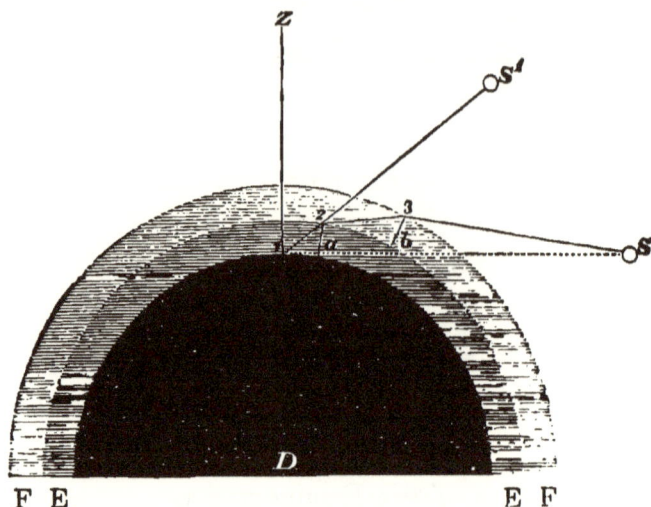

F E   E F

Let S represent the sun, D the earth, and F and E
two strata of the atmosphere of which E is the more
dense.

Ask the pupil to observe,

(*a*) That if a ray of light from *S* enter the stratum F
at **3,** it will be bent toward the perpendicular **3b,** and
enter the stratum E at **2.** The stratum E being more
dense than the stratum F, it is again bent toward the
perpendicular **2a,** and strikes the surface of the earth at **1.**

(*b*) That the atmosphere is not made up, as represented
in the diagram, of separate strata of different densities,
but becomes gradually more dense the nearer it is to the
surface of the earth. Hence, the rays of light in passing
through the atmosphere curve gradually toward a perpendicular to the surface of the earth from the point
where they enter the atmosphere.

(*c*) That there is no refraction when a ray of light
strikes the atmosphere perpendicularly, as shown by the
line **1z,** and that the more obliquely a ray enters, the
greater the refraction, as shown by the line **1 3 S.** Hence

light coming from any heavenly body in our zenith undergoes no refraction, and as a body moves from the zenith to the horizon the refraction increases.

(*d*) That since all objects are seen in the direction in which the light from them falls upon the retina of the eye, the sun **S** in the diagram is seen by an observer at **1** in the direction of **S1**. In consequence of this effect of refraction no heavenly body, unless in the zenith, is seen in its real position.

In the case of the sun and moon, the amount of refraction at the horizon is a little greater than their apparent diameters. Hence, in rising or setting, they appear above the horizon when they are actually below it.

42. The **Radiation** of heat with reference to the earth is the emission and diffusion of heat from its surface into the atmosphere.

Ask the pupil to observe,

(*a*) That during the day the surface of the earth is heated by the rays of the sun.

(*b*) That when the sun sets the earth radiates its heat into the atmosphere ; hence the change in the temperature before the sun rises.

In the summer season the earth's surface absorbs or takes in more heat from the sun during the long day than it radiates or gives out during the short night, the temperature must for this reason rise. When the sun leaves us and goes south our days shorten and nights lengthen, during which absorption diminishes, radiation increases, and the temperature is correspondingly lowered.

The blacksmith puts the horseshoe into the forge that

it may *absorb* heat until it gets soft, so that he can easily shape it upon the anvil ; while working with it the shoe *radiates* heat, getting thereby more and more difficult to work. It must soon be replaced in the forge again to absorb the required quantity of heat to be easily and economically wrought ; when the smith is through with the shoe he drops it into his tub of water that it may quickly radiate the heat and be ready to nail to the horse's hoof.

Distribution of Light and Heat.

To Illustrate the difference between the Sun's Vertical and Oblique Rays.

Take two pieces of cardboard about a foot square. In the center of one of them cut a round hole about one inch in diameter ; hold this one up to the sun at a right angle to the rays, so that the light will pass through the opening ; place the other piece about a foot behind the first and parallel to it ; ask the pupils to observe that the sunlight passing through the inch opening falls upon the second piece vertical to it, and covers a like surface of one inch. This illustrates how the sunlight, falling *vertically* upon the earth, covers a surface *equal* to the *volume* of *such light.*

Change the position of the back piece of cardboard *slowly*, so that it will *not* be parallel to the first, and ask the pupils to observe that while no more sunlight passes through the opening in the *first* cardboard than in the other illustration, yet that amount is spread over a *greater surface* on the second piece, owing *entirely* to the fact that it now falls *obliquely ;* whereas, in the first instance, it fell vertical to the surface of the cardboard. This illustrates how the sunlight, falling *obliquely* upon the earth's surface, covers a space *greater* in area than the volume of the light. Observe also, that the *greater* the obliquity, the *greater* the space covered.

Remove the second piece of cardboard, and put the globe in its place in such a manner that the sunlight admitted through the first cardboard shall fall vertical to the surface upon the equator. Observe that the area of light on the surface of the globe is about equal to the area of the hole admitting the light. Raise the cardboard so that the sunlight will fall upon the 40th parallel of north latitude, and observe that while no more sunlight is *admitted*, it covers a *much greater area*, and must be less intense there than on the equator where the sun was vertical. In the same manner place the sunlight on the 60th parallel, and observe the greater obliquity and the greater area covered. Call special attention to the fact that the *curvature* of *the globe* is the only cause of the rays in the *higher* latitude being *more* oblique than they are in the *lower* latitudes.

Observe, that what is true of a small globe and a portion of sunlight, is true of our earth as a sphere, and the greater volume of sunlight.*

Thus we find—

1. That the *nearer* the vertical sun, the more intense the light and heat ; and the *farther* from the vertical sun, the less intense the light and heat.

The cause of the heat of summer and cold of winter is not more due to the angle at which the rays of sunlight strike us, than to the relative lengths of day and night at these seasons. In midsummer we are about 15 hours in sunlight, wherein we are warming, and about 9 hours are turned away in darkness to cool, while in midwinter we have about 9 hours of sunlight and 15 hours of darkness. As we depend upon sunlight for heat, it follows that the temperature must rise in summer and fall in winter, owing to the longer and shorter periods of sunshine at these respective seasons.

2. That only *one-half* of the earth's surface can at any time, be exposed to the sun's light and heat. This half is called the *Illuminated Hemisphere.*

Rotate the globe on its axis from *west* to *east* 10 degrees, and ask the pupils to observe, in case the earth moves in like manner :

(*a*) That a distribution of light and heat will have taken place.

(*b*) That the vertical rays of the sun will have been carried *westward* 10 degrees upon the earth's surface, owing to this rotation to the *east;* or, the sun's vertical ray will have been *distributed* east and west 10 degrees.

(*c*) That the boundary of sun's light and heat will have been carried *westward* from 90 degrees west longitude to 100 degrees, and that all places situated between these

---

*NOTE.—If convenient, place a convex lens over the aperture in the cardboard ; place the second board behind, as directed in the first instance, and at such a distance as necessary to make the converging rays cover the least possible surface ; hold the sunlight upon the same point for a few moments ; and if the lens is a good one, combustion will ensue at the point of contact, thus illustrating the intense heat produced by *reducing* the space covered by a given portion of sunlight. *The intensity of solar heat is inversely proportional to the space covered by a given volume.*

meridians will have been by this distribution brought *into* the illuminated hemisphere, while those places situated between the 90th and 80th meridians *east* longitude will have been carried *out* of it.

(*d*) That the Day and Night Circle is parallel with the meridians as they pass under it.

Rotate the globe once upon its axis from west to east, and ask the pupils to observe :

(*a*) That by reason of this rotation the sun has crossed every meridian and returned to the place of starting.

(*b*) That every meridian has passed through the illuminated and the dark hemispheres. Hence, one complete distribution of light and heat *east* and *west* has taken place, being produced by the rotation of the earth upon its axis. As the earth turns once upon its axis daily, there must occur a *daily distribution of light and heat east and west upon the earth's surface.* •

(*c*) That when the sun is vertical to the equator, as on March 20th and September 23rd, the light and heat of the sun is *equally* distributed in the north and south hemispheres.

To Illustrate the Distribution of Light and Heat on March 20th.

To produce a *distribution* of the sun's light and heat upon the earth's surface, the earth or sun must change their position in respect to the other. This necessitates a *movement*, and without a movement no *distribution* can take place.

It is very necessary that the pupils get a clear conception of this subject and *master* it, as upon the distribution of light and heat depend the succession of day and night, the twilights, change of seasons, and, in fact, our *very existence.*

Bring the calendar index to the 20th of March ; rotate the globe upon its axis until the sun is vertical to the *prime* meridian, and ask the pupils to observe :

(*a*) That the sun is vertical to the equator.

(*b*) That the sun's light and heat extend north and south from pole to pole, as shown by the Day and Night Circle B.

(*c*) That the sun's light and heat extend *east* and *west* of the prime meridian 90 degrees, as shown by the Day and Night Circle B.

To Illustrate the Distribution of Light and Heat on the 21st of June.

Bring the calendar index to the 21st of June, and ask the pupils to observe :

(*a*) That the sun is vertical to the Tropic of Cancer, 23½ degrees *north* of the equator.

(*b*) That the Illuminated Hemisphere now extends 23½ degrees *beyond* the north pole, and that it fails to reach the south pole by the same number of degrees.

(*c*) That the place upon the earth's surface where the vertical ray falls, is the center of the Illuminated Hemisphere, and that any change in position of this point produces a *like* change in the *Illuminated,* and an opposite change in the *Dark* Hemispheres.

(*d*) That on June 21st the light and heat of the sun is *unequally* distributed in the north and south hemispheres ;

that the Illuminated Hemisphere predominates north of the equator, and the Dark Hemisphere predominates south of it.

Rotate the globe upon its axis, and ask the pupils to observe :

(*a*) That the vertical sun traces the Tropic of Cancer.

(*b*) That as the earth rotates upon its axis, in this manner, all places within the *Arctic* circle will *remain* in sunlight, while corresponding places within the *Antarctic* will remain *without* sunlight.

(*c*) That from the 20th of March to the 21st of June, the vertical sun has been carried north 23½ degrees, or that a north and south distribution to the extent of 23½ degrees has taken place.

To Illustrate the Distribution of Light and Heat on the 23d of September.

Bring the calendar index to the 23d of September ; this illustrates the relationship that exists between the earth and sun on that day. Ask the pupils to observe :

(*a*) That the vertical sun has, from the 21st of June to the 23d of September, been carried *south* from the Tropic of Cancer to the equator ; and that the Illuminated Hemisphere has been correspondingly changed, so that on September 23d, the sun's light and heat is again *equally* distributed in the north and south hemispheres, and extending from pole to pole, as on March 20th.

(*b*) That whatever distribution was shown, or whatever observations could be made on March 20th, are again reproduced on September 23d.

To Illustrate the Distribution of Light and Heat on December 22d.

Bring the calendar index to the 22d of December, and ask the pupils to observe :

(*a*) That the sun is vertical 23½ degrees *south* of the equator.

(*b*) That the Illuminated Hemisphere now extends 23½ degrees beyond the *south* pole, and that it fails to reach the north pole by the same number of degrees.

(*c*) That, on December 22d, the light and heat of the sun is again *unequally* distributed in the north and south hemispheres, and that the Illuminated Hemisphere predominates *south* of the equator, and the Dark Hemisphere predominates *north* of it.

Rotate the globe upon its axis, and ask the pupils to observe :

(*a*) That the vertical sun traces the Tropic of *Capricorn*

(*b*) That as the earth rotates upon its axis in this manner, all places within the *Antarctic* circle *remain* in sunlight, while corresponding places within the *Arctic* circle will remain *without* sunlight.

(*c*) That from the 23d of September to the 22d of December the vertical sun has been carried south 23½ degrees, or that a north and south distribution has taken place.

Bring the calendar index slowly to starting point (March 20th,) and observe : That the vertical sun is carried from the Tropic of Capricorn to the equator, the place of beginning; and that a north and south distribution of the sun's light and heat has taken place from the equator to both tropics and return, and that the time necessary to do this is one year ; and, *as the vertical ray is distributed, so must all other rays that touch the earth's surjace be affected.*

Thus we see that there is a *double* distribution : east and west *daily*, and north and south *annually*.

The Causes of the Existing Distribution of Light and Heat.

1. The daily distribution east and west is caused by the daily rotation of the earth on its axis.

2. The annual distribution north and south is caused:

(*a*) *By the revolution of the earth in its orbit around the sun.* If the earth remained fixed in its orbit, and revolved upon its axis, but one distribution could take place—the daily.

(*b*) *By the inclination of the earth's axis.* Notice that on the 20th of March the axis is inclined 23½ degrees, but that the inclination is *neither to* nor *from* the sun, and that the sun is then vertical to the equator. Notice that on the 21st of June the *north* pole is inclined *to* the sun the *full inclination* of 23½ degrees, and for this reason the sun is vertical the *same* number of degrees north of the equator. On December 22d, the north pole is inclined *from* the sun the full inclination, this bringing Capricorn under the sun. Erect the axis by supporting the globe on the other socket, call the pupil's attention to the fact that the equator and the ecliptic now lie in the same plane. Revolve the earth around the sun and observe that the vertical ray falls constantly upon the equator ; without an inclination no annual distribution of light and heat could take place.

(*c*) *By the parallelism of the earth's axis.* The axis is said to be parallel, because it points continually to the same part of the heavens : thus, the north pole points constantly towards the North Star, while the earth re· volves around the sun. Revolve the globe around the arc S and observe that the *axis* points constantly in the same direction. This is true of the earth and all the planets as they revolve in their several orbits. This is termed the parallelism of the axis.

Equal Days and Nights.

1. Bring the calendar index to the 20th of March, and ask the pupils to observe :

(*a*) That the Day and Night Circle B divides the earth into two divisions—day and Night : that all places on the side of this circle *next to the sun* have day, while those places on the opposite side have night.

(*b*) That at this season of the year the sun is vertical to the equator, and the Day and Night Circle is parallel to opposite meridians.

(*c*) That in *this* position the Day and Night Circle divides every parallel of latitude, from pole to pole, into *two equal* parts.

Rotate the globe slowly upon its axis, and ask the pupils to observe :

(*a*) That *all* places upon a given meridian enter the sunlight at the *same moment.*

(*b*) That *one-half* a rotation on the axis carries these

places *through* the Illuminated Hemisphere, where they pass beyond the Day and Night Circle, when the day *ends* and night *begins*.

(*c*) That one-half a rotation carries these places from sunset to sunrise.

Thus we see that on March 20th, the days and nights *must be equal* all over the earth's surface.

Bring the calendar index to the 23d of September, and ask the pupils to notice that the same condition that existed on March 20th, again exists, with the same result— equal days and nights.

Unequal Days and Nights.

Bring the calendar index to the 21st of June, and ask the pupils to observe :

(*a*) That the sun is vertical 23½ degrees *north* of the equator, and that the sunlight extends 23½ degrees *beyond* the north pole, and fails to reach the south pole by the same number of degrees.

(*b*) That the Day and Night Circle no longer divides the parallels of latitude into equal parts, but into two *unequal* parts ; and that north of the equator the *greater* part of every parallel is in the sunlight, and the *lesser* part in darkness ; while south of the equator the *lesser* part is in sunlight, and the *greater* part in darkness.

(*c*) That the entire parallels within 23½ degrees of the *north* pole are now in constant *day*, while those within the same distance of the *south* pole are in continual night.

Rotate the globe on its axis, and ask the pupils to observe :

(*a*) That no sunlight or day reaches that portion of the earth's surface within the Antarctic circle, although the earth may revolve upon its axis.

(*b*) That the entire area of the earth's surface within the Arctic circle, is not carried *out* of the sunlight by the rotation of the earth upon its axis.

(*c*) That the Day and Night Circle cuts the *equator* at opposite points, and that *there* the days and nights are equal.

(*d*) That, as you proceed *north* from the equator to the Arctic circle, the days *increase* in length gradually from 12 hours at the equator, to 24 hours within the Arctic Circle.

(*e*) That, as you proceed *south* from the equator to the Antarctic circle, the days *decrease* in length gradually, from 12 hours at the equator, to 0 hours within the Antarctic Circle.

Bring the calendar index to the 22d of December, and ask the pupils to observe : that what was true of the *northern* in *June*, is now true of the *southern* hemi-sphere in *December*. Thus it is evident—

1. That when the sun is upon the equator, the days and nights are everywhere equal.

2. That when the vertical sun is one or more degrees north or south of the equator, continual *day* must exist around the pole *nearer* the sun, and continual *night* must exist around the pole *farther* from the sun ; the extent of this area of continual day and night depending upon the distance of the vertical sun north or south of the equator.

3. That the days and nights at the equator must *always* be equal.

4. That as you depart from the equator, the variation in the length of day and night *increases*, and as you approach the equator the variation becomes *less* : the *maximum* variation being in the polar, and the minimum in the equatorial regions.

5. That the length of any day upon any parallel of *north* latitude, is equal to the night following on the corresponding parallel of *south latitude.*

NOTE.—In this work we regard *day* as the time when the sun is *present*, and night as the time when he is *absent.* Night does not necessarily mean *darkness.* Night begins at sunset and ends at sunrise.

The Sun's Apparent Path.

Bring the calendar index to the 21st of June, rotate the globe on its axis until the *Ecliptic* marked upon the globe is brought under the vertical Sun. Move very slowly the calendar index through the succeeding months until it again comes to the 21st of June, and ask the pupils to notice that the vertical sun traces the ecliptic and if the earth had no *daily* rotation on its axis, that the ecliptic would mark the true path of the Sun upon the earth.

Rotate the earth upon its *axis* and ask the pupils to observe that the Sun *traces* the *Tropic of Cancer*, and that if the sun should leave behind it a thread of light, that thread would lie upon the tropic. Move the calendar index to the 22d of June, and rotate the globe upon its axis, and notice that the sun traces a line *parallel* to the Tropic of Cancer, but about ¼ of a degree south of it. In the same manner proceed with several days in

succession and observe that by reason of the rotation of
the earth upon its axis and the movement forward of
the earth in its orbit at the same time, the path of the
vertical sun will be a continuous line running from east
to west, and winding south from Cancer to Capricorn,
and returning during the year, much as a thread is wound
upon a spool.

Change of Seasons.

To produce what is called a change of season at any
place, more solar heat must fall upon that place during
one part of the year than at *another*. Within the tropics
the amount of heat received from the sun is nearly uniform throughout the year, so that very little change of
season takes place ; the greatest changes occurring in
the higher latitudes.

Bring the calendar index to the 20th of March and
ask the pupils to observe :

(*a*) That the light and heat of the sun are equally distributed in the north and south Hemispheres.

(*b*) That if the earth remained fixed in its orbit and
was rotated upon its axis, there could be no *change* of
seasons.

Bring the calendar index to the 21st of June and ask
the pupils to observe :

(*a*) That the sun is now vertical to the tropic of cancer, and that the sun's light and heat is unequally distributed in the north and south hemispheres, the north
hemisphere having the greater and the south hemisphere
the lesser amount.

(*b*) That owing to this inequality the north hemisphere is having its greatest amount of light and heat, its warmest season or Summer, and that the south hemisphere is having its coldest season or Winter.

Bring the calendar index to the 23d of September and ask the pupils to observe that the light and heat is again equally distributed north and south of the equator as in March 20th.

Bring the calendar index to the 22d of December and ask the pupils to observe that the sun is vertical to the tropic of Capricorn, the sun's light and heat being again uneqally distributed in the north and south hemispheres, the south having the greater and the north the lesser amount ; and that at this time in the year the south hemisphere is having the warmest season or Summer, while in the north it is in the coldest or Winter season.

Bring the calendar index to the 20th of March, and observe that the sun is brought to the equator *going north* and that as it *crosses*, Spring begins in the north and Autumn or Fall begins in the south hemisphere.

The Causes that produce the Change of Seasons.

The change of seasons is produced by,

(*a*) The revolution of the earth in its orbit around the sun.

(*b*) The inclination of the earth's axis to the plane of the orbit.

(*c*) The parallelism or fixed position of the earth's axis.

(*d*) The rotation of the earth upon its axis.

To illustrate that the rotation of the earth upon its axis is one of the causes that produce the changes of seasons as they now exist : bring the calendar index to the 20th of March, mark the point upon the equator where the sun is vertical at that time ; now move the calendar index slowly through the succeeding months of the year until it is again vertical to the same point. Call the pupil's attention to the fact that if the earth did *not* rotate upon its axis the sun would require one year to cross all the meridians *once*, and that in this case it would cross them from west to east instead of from east to west; that the sun would in that event rise in the *west* and set in the *east*, and our day and year would be of the same length ; and, that if this were true, the side of the earth towards the sun would be parched by the extreme heat, while the opposite side would become frozen and lifeless. So, if the earth did not rotate on her axis, no changes of seasons as they now exist could take place, nor in fact could animal or vegetable life as now constituted endure the extremes of heat and cold to which they would be subjected.

Twilights.

To show how the sun after going below the horizon continues to give reflected light, and hence, produces twilight.

The molecules of which the atmosphere is composed, reflect the light they receive from the sun, and by the light so reflected, objects are seen in the absence of direct sunlight. The atmosphere is capable of thus reflecting light a *mean* distance of 18 degrees of a *great* circle. Call the pupils' attention to the fact that the sun gives *direct* light from the point where he is vertical to the Day and Night Circle B, and that the indirect or reflected light extends to the circle C, and that the space between these circles is called the *Twilight Belt.* Hence the earth's surface as regards light is divided into three sections : 1. A hemisphere of *direct* light. 2. A belt 18 degrees wide of reflected light or twilight. 3. The remaining portion *without light.*

To Illustrate the Twilight on the 20th of March.

Bring the calendar index to the 20th of March. Call the pupil's attention to the fact that there are two twilights, Evening and Morning ; that the evening twilight deepens into darkness, while the morning twilight brightens into sunshine. Rotate the globe upon its axis and ask the pupils to observe : that places upon the earth's surface must cross the twilight belt twice in every 24 hours. Rotate the globe slowly upon its axis and ask the pupils to observe : that all places upon the *same* meridian from pole to pole pass *into* evening twilight at the *same* instant, but that those places located near the equator pass *out* of twilight *first*, and that the higher the latitude the longer the twilight continues. This variation is due :

1st. To the fact that at the equator the earth rotates *faster* than it does near the poles, for the same reason that the outer part of a wagon wheel turns faster when the wagon is in motion, than the hub.

2d. This variation is partially due to the fact that places near the equator are carried across the twilight belt in a straight line, and at *right angles* to it : while near the poles places enter the twilight at right angles with the first circle and cross the belt not in a direct line, but travel on an arc of a circle passing obliquely across the *second* circle.

From this we see that places in the higher latitudes must travel *farther* to cross the twilight belt, and at the same time, much slower than those places situated near the equator.

Locate upon the map of the globe the place where you are situated, rotate the globe upon its axis and ask the pupils to note carefully the manner this place is carried across the twilight belt. This illustrates the twilights on the 20th of March, for that place.

To Illustrate the Twilights on the 21st of June.

Bring the calendar index to the 21st of June and ask the pupils to observe :

(*a*) That the twilight belt no longer conforms to the meridians, and that no two places upon the same meridian enter the evening or emerge from the morning twilight at the same moment.

(*b*) Those places that in March cross the twilight belt at *right angles* to it, now cross it *obliquely*, so that the twilights for these places must be longer in June than in March.

(*c*) That the obliquity is *least* at the equator, and increasing as the latitude increases.

Locate upon the map of the globe the place where you are located, rotate the globe upon its axis and ask the pupils to observe that this place is carried across the twilight belt more obliquely than in March, and that the twilight must be of *longer duration.*

To Illustrate the Twilight on the 23d of September.

'Bring the calendar index to the 23d of September, examine the twilight in the same manner as upon the 20th of March, and ask the pupils to notice that all the facts are the same as were observed at that date.

To Illustrate the Twilight on the 22d of December.

Bring the calendar index to the 22d of December, and ask the pupils to notice that places upon the earth's surface are carried across the twilight belt *obiquely* substantially as in *June.*

Compare the twilights of any place* at different dates by use of the globe, taking the 21st of June as the basis of comparison, and repeat the comparison until the pupils see clearly,

(*a*) That on the 21st of June the given place crosses the *Twilight Belt* more obliquely than on either of the other dates, and hence the longest twilight.

(*b*) That on the 20th of March and 23d of September, the path of the given place across the *Twilight Belt is* the same, and less oblique than at either of the other dates, and hence the shortest twilight.

(*c*) That on the 22d of December the given place crosses the *Twilight Belt* less obliquely than on the 21st

*The author would suggest that the place selected be in north latitude 40 to 50 degrees.

of June, and more obliquely than on the 20th of March
and 23d of September.　Hence, a mean twilight between
the other two.

3d.　Now ask the pupils to notice that on the 22d of
December the sun is vertical to south latitude 23½, and
on the 21st of June, north latitude 23½. Consequently
the sun sustains the same relation in every particular to
the Southern Hemisphere at the former date, that it does
at the latter date to the Northern.　Hence, all the facts
observed regarding the twilight on the 21st of June in
northern latitudes apply on the 22d of December to corresponding southern latitudes.　Hence, all the facts observed on the 22d of December in northern latitudes may
be found on the 21st of June in the southern latitudes.

Sun's Declination.

The Sun's Declination is his distance north or south
of the equator (as indicated by the vertical ray).　When
the sun is *north* of the equator he is said to have a *northern* declination ; when *south* of the equator he is said to
have a *southern* declination.

The greatest northern declination (23½ degrees) occurs on the 21st of June, and the greatest southern declination (23½ degrees) occurs December 22d.　At the
time of the *equinoxes* (March 20 and September 23d),
the sun has *no* declination.

To Find the Sun's Declination for any Day.

Bring the calendar index to the given day, rotate the
globe upon its axis until the meridian having the degrees
upon it is brought under the pointer L.　Extend the

pointer L to the globe. The degree of latitude under the pointer is the required Declination.

To Find the Longitude of any Place.

Rotate the globe upon its axis until the given place is under the pointer H, the degree on the equator at the end of the pointer H is the longitude required. The longitude is east or west according as the place is east or west of the Prime Meridian.

EXAMPLES.

1. What is the longitude of New York ?
2. What is the longitude of Calcutta ?
3. What is the longitude of Quito ?
4. What is the longitude of St. Petersburg ?
5. What is the longitude of Honolulu ?

To Find the Latitude of any Place.

Rotate the globe upon its axis until the given place is brought under the pointer H, above the place *on* the pointer read the degree of latitude required ; or, bring the given place under the edge of circle B, mark the circle directly over the given place, rotate the globe until the meridian having the degrees marked upon it is brought under the circle. Under the point marked, read upon the meridian the degree of latitude required. If the place is north of the equator it is north latitude, if south of it, south latitude.

EXAMPLES.

1. What is the latitude of New York ?
2. What is the latitude of Calcutta ?
3. What is the latitude of Quito ?
4. What is the latitude of St. Petersburg ?
5. What is the latitude of Honolulu ?
6. What is the latitude of Santiago ?

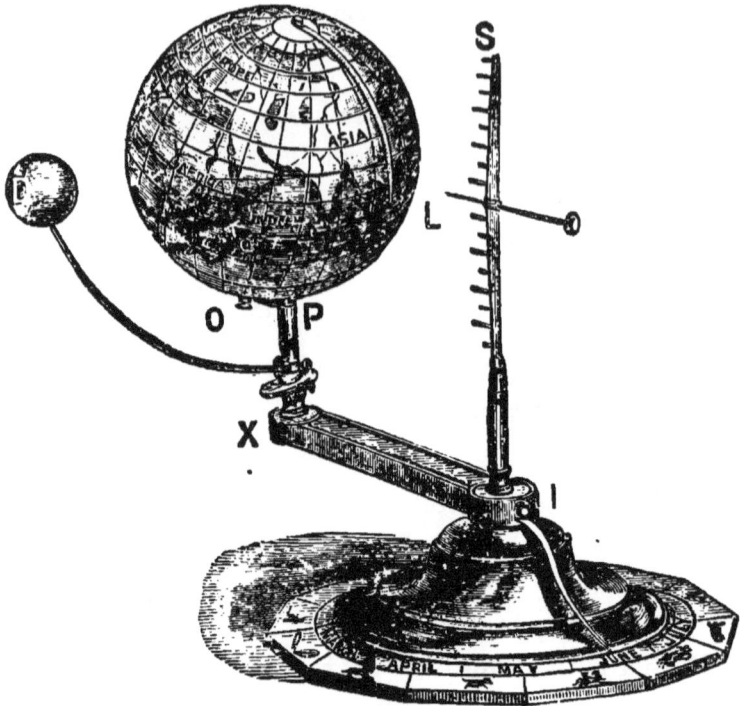

CUT No. 2.

THE LUNAR TELLURIAN
With its Day and Night Circle removed.

O is the Inclination Arm which carries the Earth globe.
P, Standard coinciding with the axis of the Ecliptic.

The Andrews Lunar Tellurian, arranged thus, is the best apparatus for explaining the phases of the moon, eclipses, equation of time, precession of the equinoxes, etc.

Longitude and Time.

Longitude is distance, measured however in degrees, minutes and seconds, east or west of a given meridian called the Prime Meridian. Observe that the degrees are marked upon the globe at the equator, east and west from the meridian of Greenwich—the Prime Meridian. On page 9 we learned that *every* circle is divided into 360 equal parts called degrees, every degree is subdivided into 60 equal parts called minutes, and every minute is subdivided into 60 equal parts called seconds. The earth in its relation to the sun turns once on its axis (360 degrees) every 24 hours, and must turn as many degrees every hour as 24 is contained times in 360 or 15 degrees. Since it turns 15 degrees in one hour, to turn *one* degree it will require 1-15 of an hour or 4 minutes of time.

Rotate the globe from west to east until the pointer L is over the prime meridian ; noon now takes place upon that meridian from pole to pole. Observe that all places *east* of this meridian have passed the sun and that their noon has passed, while those places to the *west* have not yet been brought to the sun, and *their* noon will not yet have taken place.

EXAMPLE 1.

When it is noon (12 o'clock) at Greenwich, what is the time in Hamburg, say 10 degrees east of Greenwich ? Hamburg being *east* of Greenwich the time is later by the time required by the earth to turn 10 degrees. Since the earth turns one degree in 4 minutes, to turn 10 degrees will require 10 times 4 minutes or 40 minutes. The difference in time is therefore 40 minutes, and since it is 12 o'clock at Greenwich, it is 40 minutes after 12 at Hamburg, or 20 minutes to 1 P. M.

EXAMPLE 2.

When it is noon at Greenwich what is the time at Rio Janeiro, Brazil, 52 degrees west ?

Rio Janeiro being *west* the time is earlier by the time required by the earth to turn 52 degrees. Since the earth turns 1 degree in 4 minutes, to turn 52 degrees will require 52 times 4 minutes, or 208 minutes. Reduced = 3 hours 28 minutes ; the time before noon at Rio Janeiro 12 o'clock noon less 3 h. 28 min. = 8 o'clock 32 min. A. M. the time at Rio Janeiro.

EXAMPLE 3.

When it is 11 o'clock A. M. at Hamburg what is the time at Charleston, S. C., 80 degrees west ? Charleston being west the time is *earlier.* Charleston is 80 degrees west of Greenwich and Hamburg 10 degrees east, the distance between Charleston and Hamburg is therefore 80 degrees + 10 degrees = 90 degrees ; 1 deg. = 4 min. 90 deg. = 90 × 4 = 360 minutes, reduced, = 6 hours. 11 o'clock A. M., less 6 hrs. = 5 o'clock A. M.

EXAMPLE 4.

When it is 10 o'clock A. M., at Constantinople, 28 degrees east, what is the time in Hong Kong, 112 degrees east ? Hong Kong being 112 degrees east and Constantinople being 28 degrees east, the distance between them is 112 deg. less 28 deg. = 84 deg.; 1 deg. = 4 min.; 84 deg. = 84 × 4 = 336 min.; reduced = 5 hrs. 36 min. difference in time. Hong Kong being *east*, the time there is *later* than 10 o'clock A. M. by 5 hrs. 36 min.; 10 hrs. + 5 hrs. 36 min. = 15 hrs. 36 min. or as commonly read, 3 hrs. 36 min. P. M.

EXAMPLE 5.

When it is 11.30 A. M. at San Francisco, 122 deg. west, what is the time at Melbourne, Australia, 143 deg. east? Ans. 5 hrs, 10 min. A. M. Observe that the greatest longitude a place can have is 180 deg., that is, *half way* around the earth from the prime meridian. If a person start at the prime meridian and go west he will be in west longitude until he reaches 180 degrees, when his longitude is *either* east or west. If he proceed on his course ten degrees, his longitude is 180 degrees east, less 10 degrees, or 170 East. If a companion had gone 10 degrees *east* his longitude would be 180 degrees west less 10 degrees, or 170 West; the men are manifestly 20 degrees apart.

To Find the Difference in Longitude Between Two Places.

1. If both places are in the same longitude either east or west, deduct the less from the greater and the result is their difference.

2. If one place is east and the other west, the *sum* of their longitudes is the difference, provided the sum does not exceed 180 degrees.

3. If one place is east and the other west, and the sum of their longitudes exceeds 180 degrees, deduct the amount from 360 degrees, and the remainder is the difference of longitude sought.

Suppose James and Howard leave the prime meridian, james going west and Howard going east; when each has traveled 80 degrees they are 160 degrees apart, which is their difference in longitude, Howard being *east* of James. Let each proceed 10 degrees farther and

they are 180 degrees apart, on opposite meridians, Howard being either *east* or *west* of James. Let them continue in their course 10 degrees ; James is then 100
degrees west and Howard 100 degrees east. Together
they have traveled 200 degrees, and as 360 degrees are
all there is to travel, 360 — 200 = 160, the number of
degrees between them, Howard being now 160 degrees
west of James.

Let us presume they started on their journey at noon,
and that they carried accurate time pieces ; when they
had traveled 15 degrees James would find his watch an
hour too fast, and to correct it he must turn it back,
while Howard's watch is found to be an hour too slow
and must be set ahead. To keep the watches right, these
changes must be made constantly, James turning his
watch back 4 minutes for every degree traveled, and
Howard setting his ahead in the same proportion. When
each has traveled 80 degrees as above, and it is noon at
the prime meridian, James' watch shows 6 hrs. 40 min.
A. M. (80 × 4 = 320 min. = 5 hrs. 20 min. subtracted
from 12 noon = 6 hrs. 40 min. A. M.) and Howard's
watch shows 5 hrs. 20 min. P. M. When each has traveled 90 degrees, James has 6 o'clock A. M. and Howard
6 o'clock P. M. when it is noon at the prime meridian.
When each has traveled 179 degrees, James' watch shows
4 minutes A. M., and Howard's shows 11 hrs. 56 min. P. M.
When they meet at 180 degrees their watches show the
same hour, 12, midnight. James has gained 12 hours by
setting his watch back, while Howard has lost 12 hours
by setting his ahead. Though both watches indicate the
same hour there is really a day's difference in their time.
Were they quick-witted Hibernians, we might readily

imagine them addressing each other somewhat like this: Hello! faix, its *to-day* wid me, but it's *yesterday* with you. It's nayther, sir, the other replies. It's *to-day* wid me and *to-morrow* wid you.

To Find the Time of Sunrise for any Place or any Day in the Year.

Arrange the globe as shown in Cut No. 1. Bring the calendar index to the given day, rotate the globe upon its axis until the given place is under the western edge of the day and night circle ; place the time index H opposite zero on the equator ; tighten the screw to hold it firmly in position. Turn the globe upon its axis from west to east, until place mentioned is opposite the pointer L ; note on the equator the number of degrees of longitude that has passed under the pointer, reduce the longitude to time (as directed in Longitude and Time, page 37). The result is the time from sunrise to noon, which subtracted from 12 o'clock noon, gives the hour of sunrise.

EXAMPLES.

1. What is the time of sunrise at Chicago, May 1 ?
2. What is the time of sunrise at New Orleans, June 30.
3. What is the time of sunrise at Melbourne, January 10 ?

To Find the Duration of Twilight for any Place on any Day in the Year.

Arrange the globe as above. Bring the calendar index to the given day, and the given place to the beginning of twilight. Set the index H opposite zero on the equator ; rotate the globe upon its axis until the given place is carried across the twilight belt ; note the number of degrees on the equator the globe has turned, which reduce to time, and the result is the duration of twilight required.

EXAMPLES.

1. What is the length of twilight at San Francisco, August 1 ?

2. What is the length of twilight at Berlin, June 21 ?

The Sun.

The sun is the center of our solar system, and around him all the planets revolve and from him receive their light and heat.   In matter he is 750 times greater than all the planets combined.   As all bodies attract each other and in proportion to the amount of matter they contain, so the sun's attraction must be 750 times greater than the combined attraction of all the planets, and were they all to unite they could not move him his own diameter from the center of gravity of our solar system. So we may justly regard the sun as the center of gravity. The attraction of the sun is so much greater than the earth's, that a boy weighing 75 lbs. on the earth would weigh over a ton if placed upon the sun.

The ancients thought the sun to be an immense globe of iron heated to a white heat.   While this is not literally true, it shows they had a better idea of the sun than of the earth, which they thought to be *flat*.

The apparent diameter of the sun is about ½ a degree—rather more than less.   When viewed through a powerful telescope his surface presents a mottled appearance, which Professor Newcomb likens to a dish of rice soup with the rice grains floating upon the surface.

The sun seems to be surrounded by a very rare, light atmosphere, principally hydrogen heated to a glow, in which fleecy clouds seem to float ; these clouds serve to cut off from us some of the fierce light and heat of the sun, and were it not for these, astronomers tell us his light and neat would be intolerable.

The prevailing opinion of the best authorities is, that the sun proper is composed of condensed gases under great pressure, and heated to a temperature many times greater than furnace heat.

The solar spectrum shows the presence of hydrogen, iron, magnesium, sodium and other elements in the sun ; but of what the sun is composed we know very little. His extreme brightness renders observations very difficult. If the sun were placed at the distance of the nearest fixed star he would appear no larger than one of the smaller stars.

The Sun has three motions, as follows :

1. A rotation upon his axis once in 25 days, 9½ hours.

2. A revolution around the center of gravity. This movement is very slight.

3. A revolution around some distant and unknown center, carrying with him the entire solar system at a rate of 20,000 miles an hour, and traveling in an orbit so great that to make one complete revolution requires about *eighteen million years!* This is perhaps the most astounding of all astronomical movements, and the question " Whither are we going?" may well be asked !

The Earth.

The Earth is one of the eight principal planets. She ranks fifth in size, and third in her distance from the sun. Her distance varies between 91 and 94 million miles. She has at least eight distinct motions, but some of them it is not our province to consider in this work. Among the simpler and better understood of the number are :

1. Rotation upon her axis every 24 hours.

2. Revolution around the sun annually in an Elliptical orbit.

3. Revolution of the equator around the pole of the Ecliptic. (See Precession of the Equinoxes.)

The Earth's surface is divided into solid and liquid, there being about 3-10 of the former and 7-10 of the latter. The solid we call land and the liquid water. The crust and liquid covering of the earth as compared with her size is *very thin*, probably not a hundred miles thick, and if shown upon the globe the crust would be reduced to the thickness of thin cardboard! This crust is supposed to float on the molten fiery interior of the earth. Among the proofs that the interior of the earth is a sea of fire, are the following :

1. As we go down into the solid crust of the earth the temperature rises at nearly the uniform rate of 1 degree for every 50 feet we descend. At a distance of less than 2 miles, water would boil; at a depth of 10 miles, the crust would be red-hot. Below the surface, 90 to 100 miles, the temperature would be sufficient to melt any substance known to man.

2. In various parts of the earth's surface we find springs of hot water boiling up out of the earth's crust, and we know of no way the water could be heated except by the internal fires of the earth.

3. Volcanoes, that seem to act as safety valves, through which the Furies of the pent up fires find relief in sending forth fire, gases and lava. The latter is composed of well known substances, such as rock and minerals melted to a liquid form.

4. The *form* of the earth flattened at the poles and bulged out at the equator, shows that the earth in her childhood (if we may be allowed the term), must have been in a soft, pliable state, in which case the earth would necessarily assume the form she now has. From what we know of the interior of the earth it could not have been in this soft plastic state except by the action of *heat*. Geological formations show evidences of great heat at some former period of the earth's existence.

The Moon.

The Moon's Form, Size and Physical Condition.

The moon, like the earth, is very nearly round. Her diameter is 2,160 miles, and her volume is about 1-49 the size of the earth, and only $\frac{1}{70,000,000}$ times the size of the sun. The moon, to us, *appears* nearly as large as the sun. This is because she is about 400 times nearer to us. A ball thrown high in the air seems smaller than when tossed up but a few feet. Thus we see the apparent size of bodies depends largely upon their distance from us.

The moon, as seen through a telescope, presents a very uneven and broken surface, showing very high mountains, deep valleys, and the craters of immense volcanoes now extinct. The clouded or mottled appearance of its surface sometimes called "The man in the moon," and which many ignorant people think to be land and water, is really due to the difference in the reflecting power of the various portions of the moon's surface. The higher portions of her surface seem to be composed of lighter colored material than the lower, and they will therefore reflect more light than the darker colored and lower surface. If examined through a small telescope or field glass, we are able to see some spots on the lighter sections brighter than the surrounding surface ; these are the summits of mountains, the most prominent being craters of volcanoes. The most careful observations of the moon fail to show any atmosphere. There can be no water, for the sun's heat during the long lunar days (about a month long) would evaporate it and produce a cloud-like film around the moon that could readily be seen.

The results of observations upon the physical conditions of the moon are such that we must conclude that it is a cold, lifeless body, the essential elements of life, air and water, not being found.

The Moon's Motions.

The moon has three positive motions.

1. *A revolution on her axis once in* 29½ *days.* Thus we see the lunar day is 29½ times longer than the terrestrial. To an observer, on the moon near its equator, the sun would rise in the east and set in the west ; but the

period of time between sunrise and sunset would be equal
to nearly 15 of our terrestrial days, and when the sun
had set it would not rise for an equal period. How great
must be the extremes of temperature! The lunar day
must be hotter than anything experienced upon the
earth, while, during the lunar night the temperature must
fall to a degree unknown save in the polar latitudes of
our earth. To an observer on the moon, the earth would
look like a huge moon 13 times larger than the moon
appears to us. It would present the phases of the moon
as we see them, but on a grander scale. Owing to the
moon's slow axial rotation, the earth would not appear to
revolve around it, but merely swing back and forth
through a few degrees.

2. A revolution around the earth once in 27⅓ days.

3. A revolution with the earth around the sun annually. The result of the last two motions makes the
actual path of the moon very peculiar. The second motion mentioned, of itself, would carry the moon around
the earth so that its path would be an ellipse; while
however, this movement is going on, the last mentioned
movement (No. 3) is also in operation and is about 30
times as rapid as the former (No. 2), making the actual
path an *irregular* curve, sometimes outside and sometimes inside the earth's orbit; but its path *always curves*
to the sun. The moon's orbital velocity is about 2,300
miles per hour, while she follows the earth in her great
orbital journey at the rate of 68,000 miles an hour—*over
a thousand miles a* minute.

If the earth were at rest in her orbit the path of the
moon would be similar to cut No. 3, (E the earth, M

the moon, the arrows showing the
direction of the moon's revolution). Since the earth is not at rest,
cut No. 3 shows the *relative* and not
the *true* path of the moon.

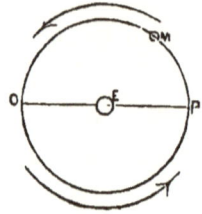

CUT No. 3.

Let A in cut 4 represent part of
the orbit of the earth, and E B F
will show the *true* path of the
moon from her last to her first
quarter, or while traveling from
O to P, as shown in cut 3. The
moon makes this path because
she is carried forward with the
earth around the sun from F to E
while she is revolving around the
earth from O to P, cut 3. If the
moon's path from F to E were on
the line G H, she would neither
curve to nor from the sun, but be
traveling on a straight line and at
right angles to him. If this were
true, at the point J, she would be
over 400,000 miles from the earth
then at I, but as the moon's dist-
tance is about 240,000 miles, she
must be at K instead of J. Hence,
the moon's path must be on the
line E B F, which is concave to,
or curving towards the sun. After
passing the point E the moon's
orbit curves sharply in, and in 14

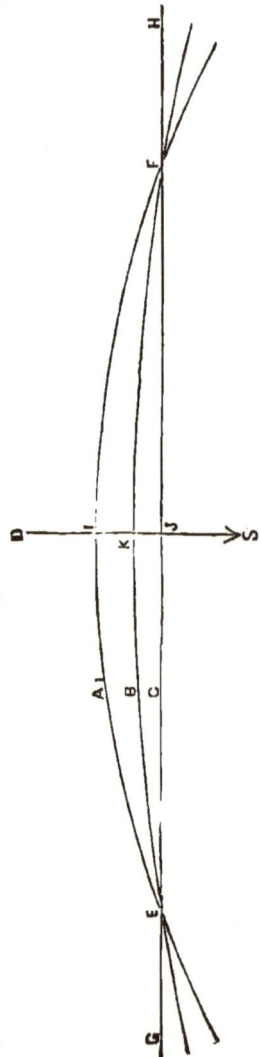

CUT No. 4

days crosses to the inside of the earth's orbit, as we observe it does at the point F.

The Sidereal and Synodic Revolutions of the Moon.

The moon revolves around the earth in an *elliptical*
orbit once in 27⅓ days ; this is called the sidereal revolution. Sidereal means Star.

Ask the pupils to observe that as the moon ball revolves around the globe it is nearer the globe when on
one side of it than when upon the other. In like manner
the moon revolves around the earth ; sometimes she ap-
proaches within 221,000 miles of the earth. Her greatest distance is 259,000. She seldom reaches these extreme limits ; her usual variations are about 13,500 miles
either way from the average, which is about 240,000 miles.

Ask the pupils to observe the position of the moon
and some star near it in the heavens ; on the following
evening the moon will have moved some distance to the
eastward ; continue the observations through several
evenings, and note the changes of the moon's position
in the stars. In 27⅓ days (about) the moon will have
passed clear around the heavens and will again appear
near the star where it was first observed. The moon has
now made one *sidereal* revolution (one revolution as regards the stars). If the sun and not a star were taken
for the base of the observation, the time required for the
moon to revolve around the earth and be brought to its
former position relative to the sun would be 29½ days,
about. This is a *synodical* revolution.

Call the pupil's attention to the fact that the sun apparently travels from *west* to *east* through the heavens,
going clear around, or 360 degrees in a year (about 365

days), and of course must travel on an average *nearly* a degree a day. The moon makes a complete revolution through the heavens in 27⅓ days, or about 13 degrees daily, and in the same direction that the sun apparently travels. Let us suppose the sun, the moon and a star to be in line on a given day ; on the day following, if observed, the sun will be seen about 1 degree east of the star, and the moon will be seen about 13 degrees east of the star and 12 degrees east of the sun. The following day the sun will be about 2 degrees east of the star and the moon will be about 26 degrees east of the star and 24 degrees from the sun. Observe that at this rate the moon will be 27⅓ days in passing around the earth and again getting into line with the star, thus completing the sidereal revolution. The sun in the mean time has passed to about 27 degrees east of the star, and for the moon to overtake him will require about 2 1-6 days additional, thus completing the synodical revolution in 29½ days. The change of the moon depends upon its relation to the *sun* and not to a star, so, from one new moon to another is 29½ days (about).

The Phases of the Moon.

The moon shines by reflected sunlight ; like the earth, one-half of her surface is illuminated by the sun, and when any part of the light hemisphere is turned toward the earth, we see that portion brightly illuminated, and the light it gives us we call moonlight. The moon acts as a great heavenly mirror reflecting the sun's light after he is gone. The bright side of the moon is of course always toward the sun.

The Dark Moon.

Ask the pupils to notice that when the moon is between the earth and sun, the light hemisphere of the moon must be hid from the earth. *Astronomically* we say the moon and sun are in conjunction ; as ordinarily expressed, we say it is the " Dark of the Moon " or " No Moon." Demonstrate this by the apparatus.

New Moon.

Move the globe forward in the orbit until the moon has passed two or three inches to the east of the pointer L. Ask the pupils to observe that the moon is not now between the globe and the arc S, but has passed to the eastward, and that now the hemisphere seen from the globe has a crescent of light around the western part and that the " Horns of the Moon " or the ends of the crescent point eastward. We say the moon is now new,* and being but little east of the sun, sets soon after him. At new moon when the air is clear we can plainly see the outline of the dark hemisphere. When the moon is situated nearly between the earth and sun as at new moon, the bright or illuminated hemisphere of the earth is towards the moon. Show this upon the apparatus mounted as in cut No. 1. An observer on the moon's dark hemisphere would now have, if we may be allowed the term, *earthlight*, in character similar, though in quantity greater than the light we receive from the moon when it is full. The sunlight reflected *by* the earth to the moon is in a diminished quantity re-reflected by her to the earth, and by this light twice reflected we see

---

*In *fact* the moon the moment she passes between the earth and sun, or reaches conjunction, becomes "new," though she is not usually called new until the crescent is visible. Hereafter, in this work New Moon means Conjunction.

dimly the moon's dark hemisphere. The reason why the moon's crescent is brighter than the dark hemisphere, is because the light coming from it is reflected but *once*, while that from the dark hemisphere is reflected *twice*, the difference in brilliancy showing the loss by the second reflection.

When new moon occurs while the moon is above the ecliptic, as shown in cut No. 1, the moon will be *above* as well as east of the sun, and her crescent must appear *lower* than when she is below the ecliptic. Thus we have what is called the " dry " and " wet " moon.

First Quarter.

Move the arm IX forward until the moon ball has passed one-fourth of the way around the globe from the arc S. To an observer on the globe the crescent of light during this movement will have increased until now one-half of the illuminated hemisphere is in view. The moon is now one-quarter of the way around the earth from the sun, and is in *quadrature*. The moon is now in her *first quarter*.

Full Moon.

Move the arm IX forward until the moon ball has passed *one-half* the way around the globe, and call the pupil's attention to the fact that an observer upon the earth would see the *entire* illuminated hemisphere of the moon, and that as she is almost directly opposite the sun she must rise at or near sunset. The moon is now in *opposition* with the sun and we have, illustrated, the phase of the moon called the *Full Moon.*

Last Quarter.

Move the arm IX forward until the moon ball has passed *three-fourths* of the way around the globe and ask the pupils to observe, as this is done, that the illuminated hemisphere of the moon shifts to the eastward so that when it is brought to the three-quarter position only one-half of it is visible to an observer upon the globe. The moon is again in quadrature with the sun, and presents the phase of the moon in her *last quarter*.

Old Moon.

Move the arm IX until the moon ball is brought about half way between the last quarter and the dark of the moon, and observe that a crescent of light may be seen around the eastern side of the moon, the horns of the crescent pointing to the *west*. The moon is now " old," from which position she passes to conjunction and the dark moon, thus completing the common phases of the moon.

The Orbit of the Moon.

The orbit of the moon is an ellipse, her least distance from the earth is 221,000 miles, while her greatest distance is 259,000 miles. She seldom, however, reaches these extreme limits, her usual variations from her mean distance of 240,000 miles, being about 13,500 miles each way. The orbit of the moon crosses the orbit of the earth at an angle a little greater than 5 degrees. This is shown (somewhat exaggerated) by plate E on the globe, which carries the moon ball in an inclined orbit above and below the ecliptic. The moon's declination is her distance north or south of the ecliptic. In cut No. 1

the moon is shown above the ecliptic in her greatest
northern declination. In cut No. 2 she is shown below
the ecliptic in her greatest southern declination.

The Moon's Nodes.

The nodes of the moon are the two points where her
orbit cuts or crosses the ecliptic. The node where the
moon crosses the ecliptic coming north is called her
ascending node, and the opposite one the descending
node.

The pupils should fix clearly the moon's nodes in their
minds, as upon this depends the understanding of much
that is to follow.

If the sun and moon could leave a thread of light to
mark their pathway through the heavens (the sun's apparent annual path), we would observe these lines running very near each other and to cross at opposite points
of the heavens, so that as viewed from the earth the path
of the sun would sometimes be above, and sometimes
below the path of the moon, crossing it at opposite points
—the moon's nodes. These points of crossing are not
fixed, but are constantly changing, falling back to the
westward on the ecliptic or sun's apparent path about 20
degrees annually. If the nodes were stationary, then
the time required by the sun to pass from one ascending
node to another, manifestly, would be a year. Because
of the moon's nodes revolving backward on the ecliptic
about 20 degrees annually, he will approach her nodes
about 19 days earlier than he otherwise would. Dis-
carding fractions we have : 1 year, 365 days, less 19 days
= 346 days the time required by the sun to pass from
one ascending node to another. As the descending node

occurs midway between two ascending nodes, we have 346 days ÷ 2 = 173 days as the time from the ascending to the descending node, and an equal period from the descending to the ascending nodes.

Move the arm IX until the moon ball is between the globe and the arc S, turn the plate E to the right until the center of the moon ball is opposite the pointer L; the sun and moon are now at the node. Note the day of the month under the calendar index G. Move the arm IX forward carrying the globe around the arc S to its former position and, at the same time, turn the plate E about 1-18 the way around in the *opposite* direction, and observe the sun has, because of this change in the position of the moon's orbit, *passed* the moon's node about 19 days earlier than he would have done had the moon's orbit not changed position·

The Zodiacal Belt.

The Zodiacal Belt is a band in the heavens lying 8 degrees on either side of the ecliptic, in which the sun, moon and the principal planets are seen to move. All the planets go around the sun in the same general direction, from west to east. The orbit of the earth, the ecliptic, is the base, and from it the inclinations of the orbits of the several planets are measured. None of the orbits of principal planets cross the orbit of the earth at an angle *greater* than 8 degrees and most of them cross at an angle considerably less. If all the planets could leave behind them a thread of light to mark their pathway through the heavens, we would see that within a belt of the heavens 16 degrees wide, lying 8 degrees on either side of the ecliptic, would lie the orbits of all

the principal planets, and in this belt they would be seen
to move. This band or zone of the heavens is called
" The Zodiacal Belt."

The Signs of the Zodiac.

The ancient astronomers for some reason not now well
known, divided the Zodiacal Belt into twelve equal parts
of thirty degrees each, giving to each sign a name, beginning with the vernal equinox or the equinoctial col-
ure, counting thirty degrees east and naming this "sign"
"Aries;" to the next thirty degrees east they gave the
name "Taurus," so continuing in the order shown upon
the base of the globe. Thus we see that a "Sign of the
Zodiac" is a portion of the heavens having a longitude
or length of 30 degrees and a latitude or breadth of 16
degrees.

Passage of the Moon Through the Signs of the Zodiac.

We learned upon the previous page that the moon had
her revolution in the Zodiacal Belt, and as she passes
clear around the heavens, 360 degrees, in making her
sidereal revolution, she must in that time have passed
once through all the Signs of the Zodiac. If the moon
passes through the 12 Signs of the Zodiac in 27⅓ days,
(a sidereal revolution), she will occupy about 2¼ days in
passing through *one* sign.

Rotate the globe upon its axis until the *ecliptic* marked
on the globe lies in a *horizontal* plane. If you were to
take a large and wide barrel hoop and place it around
the entire apparatus and hold it in such a position that
the plane of the ecliptic extended to the hoop it would
strike the middle of the hoop all the way around it; the

hoop would then show the position of the Zodiacal Belt for the Lunar Tellurian. Or, if the apparatus were placed in a large tub, and water were poured in until one-half of the globe ball only remained above the water, the surface of the water would be the plane of the ecliptic, and that portion of the tub, say 2 inches above and 2 inches below that surface would represent the Zodiacal Belt. If the tub were made of twelve wide staves, each stave would represent a " Sign of the Zodiac." Let the globe move forward in her orbit, and the moon would be seen by an observer upon the globe, to pass through these signs upon the staves from west to east, as the moon in the heavens actually does pass through, or by the Signs of the Zodiac.

When we say the moon is in Aries, we mean that the moon as seen from the earth is in that sign, or more properly, *between* us and that part of the Zodiacal Belt called the sign Aries. A very instructive and interesting illustration may be given by placing the Lunar Tellurian upon a table and having the pupils, twelve in number, join hands around it. Let each one take the name of the sign nearest to him on the base of the globe. Move the arm IX forward, and when the moon ball, in passing around the globe, comes between the globe and one of the pupils, let that pupil speak the name of the sign he represents ; thus, Mary will say, when the moon ball is opposite her, "Aries;" in a moment it has passed Mary and is opposite John, who calls out, " Taurus," and so on through the twelve signs. Where the pupils join hands will mark the divisions of the signs.

The writer strongly urges the use of the above illustration, for by it the children, though quite small, will get a very clear conception of the Zodiacal Belt, the signs of the Zodiac and the way the moon passes through these signs.

Passage of the Sun Through the Signs of the Zodiac

The sun passes through the signs of the Zodiac in a. manner very similar to the moon, and the illustrations used to show the passage of the moon through the signs may be used to equal advantage to show the sun's passage. The sun passes through the twelve signs once every year and so occupies about one month in passing each sign. The pointer G, cut No. 1, shows at all seasons of the year the sign and the degree of the sign where the sun is situated. Thus, at the vernal equinox we see the sun is in the first degree of the sign Aries. Move the arm IX forward to June 21, and observe that in the mean time the sun has passed *through* the signs Aries, Taurus and Gemini, and has reached the sign Cancer.

NOTE. When studying the change of seasons we saw that on June 21st the sun reached its greatest northern limit 23½ degrees north of the equator, from which position it turned southward towards the equator. Thus we see the sun turns south at the moment he reaches the sign Cancer. We derive the word "Tropic" from the Greek word *trepo*, which means to turn. The word Cancer shows the *position* of the sun *when* it turns southward, and from a union of these two we get "Tropic of Cancer." The same is true of the turning of the sun northward on December 22d, as it reaches the sign Capricornus, thereby giving us "Tropic of Capricorn."

Passage of the Earth Through the Signs of the Zodiac.

The earth is always said to be in the sign directly opposite the one where the sun is situated. Thus, when the sun is in Cancer the earth is said to be in Capricornus, where it would be seen by an observer upon the *sun's* surface.

Eclipses.

An eclipse in general, is the cutting off in whole or in part the sunlight, as it falls upon the earth or moon. All the planets are opaque ; they absorb in part the sunlight that falls upon them, and the remainder after absorption is reflected back into space. No light passes through them. They cast shadows into space, the extent of these shadows depending upon the *size* of the planet and its *distance* from the sun. The larger the planet the larger the shadow, and the farther the planet is from the sun the farther the shadow will extend into space. To illustrate this, draw a circle on the blackboard a foot in diameter to represent the sun, mark this circle S ; *two* feet from this circle draw a small circle, say three inches in diameter, mark this circle E to represent the earth. Draw a straight line from the top of circle S to the top of circle E, continue the line a foot or more *beyond* E ; next, draw a line from the bottom of circle S to the bottom of circle E, and continue this straight line until it crosses the other line ; the distance from where these lines cross, to the circle E, represents the distance the shadow of the earth would extend. Draw another three inch circle, say *four* feet away from circle S, and draw similar straight lines from top to top and bottom to bottom of the circles, extending them as in the other illustration, and ask the pupils to observe, that now the distance from the crossing of the lines to the circle E is *greater* than in the first instance when the circles were closer together. Thus we see that the nearer a body of a given size is *to* the sun the shorter will be its shadow, and the farther it is from the sun the *longer* will it extend. Draw a straight line from the center of circle S through the center of circle E, and extend it until it reaches the crossing of the two lines before mentioned, and ask the pupils to observe that the line last drawn may represent the ecliptic, and that it divides the shadow, into two equal parts, one-half of which is *above* and one-half below it. So the earth into space casts her shadow, equal parts of which lie above and below the ecliptic. Thus we see :

(*a*) That the shadows cast by any planet, great or small, must lie in the plane of that planet's orbit.

(*b*) That the shadows cast by the planets are in the shape of a *cone* tapering to a point, the base of the cone being equal in diameter to the diameter of the planet, the distance to the point or frustum of the cone depending upon the distance of the planet from the sun.

(*c*) That the diameter of the shadow at any point depends upon the distance of that point from the body casting the shadow.

The cone-shaped shadow of the planet is called its *umbra*, and to an observer situated in the umbra the sun is wholly obscured and to him the eclipse is total. Place the observer just outside of the umbra and the sun is not wholly obscured to him ; his situation is now in *penumbra*. To show the *penumbra* take the figures upon the blackboard used to show the umbra, and in addition draw a straight line from the *bottom* of circle S through the *top* of circle E and extend it a foot or two beyond. Draw another straight line from the *top* of circle S through the *bottom* of circle E and extend it as before, the space *beyond* the circle E on either side of the umbra and between it and the lines last drawn shows the penumbra. The shadows of all heavenly bodies must have umbra and penumbra.

Umbra means *totality*, and *penumbra*, *partiality*.

The Dimensions of the Earth and Moon's Umbra.

The length of the earth's umbra is about 860,000 miles, or about 3½ times farther than the moon is from the earth. This is the *average* length: in December and January (because then near the sun) the umbra is about 843,000 miles, while in June and July (when farthest away) her umbra is nearly 872,000 miles. The diameter of the earth's umbra at the distance of the moon is on an average about 6,000 miles, nearly three times the moon's diameter.

The average length of the moon's umbra is 236,000 miles. It varies, however, from 221,150 to 252,640 miles. *Observe that the average length of the moon's umbra is a little less than her average distance from the earth* (240,000 *miles*). *Therefore, if the moon having her avage umbra pass between the earth and sun at her average distance from us, the umbra would not reach the earth by nearly* 4,000 *miles.* The eclipse *in this case would be annular and not total.* (See *annular eclipses* page 66).

The greatest possible diameter of the moon's umbra as it falls upon the earth is about 175 miles, and this can be only when the moon is at her greatest distance from the sun and at her least possible distance from the earth.

Eclipses are known as solar and lunar, and as the terms indicate, they are of the sun and moon.

Lunar Eclipses may be $\left\{\begin{array}{l}\text{Partial or}\\\text{total.}\end{array}\right.$

Solar Eclipses may be $\left\{\begin{array}{l}\text{Partial, total}\\\text{or annular.}\end{array}\right.$

Lunar Eclipses.

If the moon revolved around the earth *in the plane of the ecliptic* she would pass through the earth's shadow and be eclipsed at every *full moon*, and would throw her own shadow upon the earth at every *new moon*. Her orbit is, however, inclined to the ecliptic, as shown by plate E on the globe. That she may pass through the earth's shadow and be eclipsed, the moon must, when full, be at or near her node, otherwise she will pass above or below the earth's shadow. It is not necessary that the moon be *exactly* at her node to strike the earth's shadow, for, if within 10½ degrees either before or after the node, she will pass into the earth's shadow and be wholly or partially eclipsed, according to her nearness *to* or distance *from* the node when she " fulls." This distance, 10½ degrees either way from the node, is called the " lunar ecliptic limits." Thus we see, that at either node there is a lunar eclipse limit of 21 degrees ; includ ing both nodes, 42 degrees, within which limits all lunar eclipses must occur.

Move the arm IX of the globe forward, until the moon ball is brought to " full," as shown in cut No. 2 ; loosen the screw holding plate E, and turn the plate until the gear-wheel that drives the moon ball rests upon the lower part of the plate, as shown in cut ; tighten the screw, ask the pupils to observe, that now the full moon is below the ecliptic (the line J, as marked upon the globe), and that the shadow of the earth will pass above the moon, and no eclipse will occur.

☞ *It is important that the pupils remember, that while the relative sizes of the earth, sun and moon are shown, it is impossible to show their relative distances. If we were to do this, the globe should be placed about a mile and a half from the arc S and the moon ball placed about 20 feet from the globe, and if placed at these distances, the moon ball must be at or very near the globe's ecliptic when full, in order to fall within the shadow; a little variation above or below would cause the moon ball to miss the globe's shadow altogether.*

If full moon occurs when the moon is a few degrees (say 10 degrees) before she reaches her ascending node, she will pass through the *lower* portion of the earth's shadow, thus covering the *upper* part of the moon's surface with shadow, giving a partial eclipse of the moon. Should full moon occur when the moon is 10 degrees past her ascending node, her *lower* limb or edge would be eclipsed by the higher portion of the earth's shadow. Revolve the plate E one-half way around, and ask the pupils to observe that now the moon ball is *above* the ecliptic J, and that the shadow must fall below it. If full moon occurs when the moon is at or very near her node, the entire moon will pass through the earth's shadow and the eclipse will be total. Such an eclipse occurred about midnight June 11, 1881.

Solar Eclipses.

There are but two celestial objects that can ever come

between us and the sun of sufficient size to cut off from us the solar light. These two are the moon and Venus. The passage of the planet Venus across the sun's face, is usually called a transit of Venus. A transit of Venus occurred Dec. 9, 1874. The next took place Dec. 6, 1882, since which there has been none. The next transit will occur June 8, 2004.

There are three classes of solar eclipses, viz.: total, partial, and annular. Let us treat them in their order.

All eclipses of the sun, being caused by the passage of the moon between us and the sun, *must* occur at *new moon*. Now, if new moon occur while she is in the vicinity of her node there must be an eclipse of some kind. If she is *at* or *very near* her node, she will pass across the sun's face *centrally*, or very nearly so; and if at this time she happens to be *near enough* to us, her umbra will reach some portion of the earth's surface, and to that region the eclipse will be total. On page 61 we learned that the greatest possible diameter of the moon's umbra at the earth is 175 miles; the usual region of totality is very much less. Thus we see why total eclipses of the sun are visible to so small portions of the earth's surface, while a lunar eclipse may be seen from any part of an entire hemisphere. The duration of solar eclipses is very much less than lunar. The length of totality in a solar eclipse cannot *exceed* 6 or 7 minutes, and is usually very much less, while the moon may remain totally eclipsed for nearly two hours. The apparent size of the sun and moon are very nearly the same, and it requires the *entire* body of the moon to hide the sun's disc and eclipse him wholly; sometimes she is not able to do even this, as we shall shortly see

If an observer were stationed on the *moon* during a total *lunar* eclipse, he would, from his position, see a total *solar* eclipse. To him the apparent size of the earth and sun would vary greatly, the former appearing between thirteen and fourteen times larger than the latter. The observer so stationed could not have an eclipse of the earth, as the largest shadow his little orb could cast upon us would not be half as large as the State of Illinois, and to him it would appear like a mere speck floating across the face of the earth.

Outside of the field of totality in a solar eclipse the eclipse must be partial when it is seen at all. Suppose the city of St. Louis to be near the center of the field of totality of a solar eclipse. At the moment of totality in St. Louis an observer in St. Paul would see the moon as below the sun, and in the passage by, his face would obscure only the lower portion of it ; to him the eclipse is *partial*. An observer at New Orleans would see the moon passing rather *above*, hiding only his upper limb or edge, while a person in South America could not see the eclipse at all.

Move the arm IX forward until the moon ball is brought to *new moon*, as in cut No. 1. Move the plate E until its highest point supports the moon ball, and ask the pupils to observe that now the moon is above the ecliptic J, and the shadow of the moon must fall above and not upon the earth , were they placed at their proper distance (20 feet). Move the plate E until the moon ball falls into the plane of the ecliptic, and ask the pupils to observe that the shadow of the moon in this position must fall *upon* the earth.

On page 61 we find the average length of the moon's umbra is 236,000 miles, and her average distance from the earth 240,000 miles, so, should the moon pass across the sun's face when so situated the umbra would not reach the earth by some 4,000 miles. The apparent size of the moon is now smaller than the sun, and she would in this position be unable to hide his entire face from us, and when passing by his center, a ring or fringe of light would be seen all around the moon. An eclipse of this kind is called *annular*. The word annular means like a ring or ring shaped, referring to the ring or fringe of light seen around the moon. Thus we see that the moon must be nearer the earth than her average distance, or that the sun must be at a greater than his average distance to make it possible for the moon to hide his entire face and to produce a total eclipse of the sun.

Move the arm IX forward, and ask the pupils to observe, that the apparatus shows the moon sometimes nearer the earth than at others.

It is not necessary that new moon occur exactly at the moon's nodes to give an eclipse of the sun ; if within $16\frac{1}{2}$ degrees of it *either way*, she will eclipse him. Thus we see the " *solar* ecliptic limit " is 33 degrees at either node or, in all, 66 degrees for both nodes, and within this limit must all solar eclipses occur.

Why more Solar than Lunar Eclipses.

On page 62 we see the moon must be within $10\frac{1}{2}$ degrees (either before or after) of her node at Full Moon to enter the earth shadow, consequently her Lunar Ecliptic limit is $10\frac{1}{2} + 10\frac{1}{2} = 21$ degrees at either node, or a total of 42 degrees of her orbit wherein lunar eclipses may occur. In the last section we see the *solar* ecliptic limit is 33 degrees at either node, or a total of 66 degrees in which *solar* eclipses may occur. Then it follows that the proportion of *solar* to *lunar* eclipses is the same as 66 bears to 42 or as 11 to 7.

Season of Eclipses.

We have already learned (page 55) that the time from one node to another is 173 days. If a new moon occurs near ascending node and eclipses the sun, in 173 days following, full moon will occur near the descending node and she will pass into the earth's shadow and be eclipsed. In 1881 the moon's nodes occurred about June 11 and December 1. In 1882 they occurred about 19 days earlier, or about May 22 and November 11, and so con-tinue to recede from year to year, owing to the falling back of the moon's nodes.

The *solar* ecliptic limit 33 degrees, is equal in time to 36 days. So an eclipse of the sun may occur 18 days before or 18 days after the moon's node, which, in the year 1881, extended from May 23 to June 29; while the *solar* ecliptic limit for the opposite node embraced the time from November 12 to December 18.

The *lunar* ecliptic limit 21 degrees, is equal to 23 days, thus an eclipse of the moon may take place at any full moon occurring 11½ days before or after the node. Thus the *lunar* ecliptic season was from May 30 to June 22, and from November 19 to December 12, of the year 1881.

The Period of Eclipses.

By referring to the subject of the moon's nodes (page

54) we find the nodes are not fixed, but have a retrograde movement on the ecliptic, nearly 20 degrees every year, or at a rate that will carry them clear around the ecliptic in about 18 years, 5 months. If we mark carefully the position of the nodes on the ecliptic now, and note the eclipses that occur for 18 years, 5 months, and record the result, and observe the phenomena for a like period following, we shall find the eclipses for the *latter* period almost identical with those of the first. Knowing this the astronomers are able to foretell eclipses to the very day and hour a hundred years in advance of their occurrence ! These periods are called the Saros or Period of Eclipse.

The Precession of the Equinoxes.

The precession of the equinoxes is due to a gyratory movement of the earth's axis revolving the poles of the equator around the poles of the ecliptic. As the equator or equinoctial and the ecliptic cut each other at an angle of 23½ degrees, so must their axis bisect. Upon the globe is marked the equator and ecliptic. The poles of the equator are the ends of the axis of the globe, and the poles of the ecliptic the points where a vertical line drawn through the center of the globe would cut its surface. This gyratory movement of the earth's axis is very slow, requiring about 25,800 years to complete one revolution. The effect of the movement is to carry the equinoctial and solstitial points backward, slowly, around the ecliptic from east to west. The value of this movement annually is 50.1 seconds of arc. The earth's orbit, like all circles, is divided into 360 degrees, these degrees subdivided into minutes and the minutes into seconds.

The exact solar year* is the time required by the earth to travel 360 degrees of its orbit, less 50.1 seconds, or 359 deg., 59 min., 9.9 sec. To illustrate upon the globe the precession, or more properly the *recession* of the equinoxes, proceed as follows :

1. Arrange the globe as shown in cut **2**, page 36; rotate the globe upon its axis until the ecliptic upon the globe lies in a horizontal plane.

2. Move the arm O slowly to the left, completing a circle around the standard P, and observe that as this is done the poles of the equator describe circles around the poles of the ecliptic (the north pole of the ecliptic on the globe being where the 90th meridian east crosses the arctic circle). In like manner the poles of the *earth* describe circles around the poles of the ecliptic once every 25,800 years, as before stated.

3. Adjust the globe for the calendar ; move the globe slowly forward in its orbit, and observe that the pointer *L* traces the ecliptic, crossing the equator, giving equinoxes about March 20 and September 23.

4. Move the arm O a part of the way around the standard P, as in 2 above, say one-half of an inch; move it forward in its orbit, and observe that the equinoxes do *not* occur at the same points in the orbit as in the former instance, but *earlier*. Repeat the operation, moving the

---

*Quite frequently called the Tropical Year. There are generally reckoned three years. 1. Sidereal Year, as the time required by the earth to make one complete orbital movement, or 365 days, 6 hours, 9 minutes, 9 seconds. 2. The Solar or Tropical Year, as the time required for the sun's vertical ray to pass from tropic to tropic and return, or 365 days, 5 hours, 48 minutes, 46 seconds. 3. The Civil Year of 365 and 366 days, according as the year is a common or leap year.

arm O little by little, and observe the equinoctial points falling back in the orbit as the arm O is moved.

5. The vernal equinox occurs as the sun enters the first degree of the sign Aries of the Zodiac. If these signs were fixed as regards the orbit, manifestly the next succeeding vernal equinox would occur 50 1 seconds *before* the sign Aries were reached, and so continue to fall back in the signs from year to year. The signs, however, are shifted to agree with the falling back of the equinoxes ; thus the equinoxes will always occur in the same degree and sign as now. The *signs*, however, do *not agree* with the constellations from which they derive their names.

Equation of Time.

Sidereal, Solar and Mean Time.

Time is a measurement of duration. One of the first objects of astronomical study was to find a standard for the measurement of duration. For this purpose the apparent diurnal revolution of the sun marked the beginnings and endings of the standard days ; while this did not mark duration into *uniform* periods of time, it was found to be sufficiently accurate for the civil, and the crude astronomical uses of the earlier days. The sun-dial served to mark the subdivisions of the day ; but as the dial was useless in the night time or in cloudy weather, a more reliable indicator was sought in mechanical devices, similar to our clocks and watches. The makers of these were sorely perplexed because they could not make their machines " agree with the sun " for any considerable time ; because of this, we are told, the makers suffered persecution, and their machines fell into disrepute, and were little used ; and where used at all, they merely supplemented the sun-dial, by which they were " regulated " from time to time.

It was soon discovered that the sun days were not of uniform length, and that the machines were the better time-keepers. The causes of this variation will be explained before we leave the subject.

The Sidereal Day is the period that elapses between two successive transits of any fixed star ; this period is unvarying. The length of the sidereal day is 24 sidereal hours, or 23 hours, 56 minutes, 4 seconds of "mean time."

The Solar Day is the period that elapses between two successive transits of the sun ; this period varies in length, being sometimes *more* and sometimes *less* than 24 mean time hours. Thus it is that the clock and sun do not agree.

The Mean Day or the *Mean Solar Day* is the *average* length of all the solar days of the year, and is of course unvarying in length, and is the standard civil day which our clocks and watches are made to keep. The mean day is 3 minutes 56 seconds longer than the sidereal day.

The varying lengths of the solar days depend upon two causes :

1. *The unequal velocity at which the earth travels in its orbit.*

2. *The inclination of the equator to the ecliptic.*

*1. To Illustrate that the Unequal Velocity of the
Earth in its Orbit is a Cause of the Existing
Variation of the Lengths of the Solar Days.*

Arrange the globe as shown in cut 2, page 36, and
proceed as follows :

Bring the calendar index to the 21st of June ; rotate
the globe upon its axis until the prime meridian is under
the pointer L ; extend the pointer L until it is within 1-16
of an inch of the globe. Move the globe forward in its
orbit an entire revolution, and observe that the pointer L
is by this movement carried from *west* to east across the
meridians at a rate that will carry it clear around—360
degrees—in one year of 365¼ days (about), or a trifle
less than a degree a day, on the average. This distance
is equal in *time* to 3 minutes 56 seconds.

Rotate the globe upon its axis from *west* to *east*, and
observe that this movement carries the pointer L across
the meridians from *east* to *west* at a rate that will carry
it clear around in *one* day ; so it follows that while the
daily rotation is carrying the sun's vertical ray 360 degrees from *east* to *west*, the forward movement of the
earth in its orbit is carrying it back nearly a degree
(about 59 minutes of distance), from *west* to *east*. Therefore, the earth must turn *more* than once upon its axis to
complete a solar day. This little " more " in a year
amounts to 360 degrees, a revolution. So, the truth is
apparent that the earth must turn 366 times upon its axis
to complete 365 solar days ; or 366 sidereal days are
equal to 365 solar days.

*If the movement of the earth in her orbit were uni-
form day to day throughout the year, the variation
would be uniform, and the solar days would be of equal
length.*

As the orbital movement of the earth is *not* uniform,* and the daily revolution *is* uniform, a variation in the lengths of the solar days must follow.

2. *To Illustrate that the Inclination of the Equator to the Ecliptic is a Cause of the Existing Variation in the Lengths of the Solar Days.*

Arrange the globe as shown in cut 2, page 36. Bring the calendar index to the 20th of March, rotate the globe upon its axis until the ecliptic lies in a *horizontal* plane. Ask the pupils to observe : That the equator and the ecliptic are both great circles, and that a degree of one is equal to a degree of the other. That the earth rotates in the direction of the plane of the equator. The vertical sun travels on the ecliptic. *a*, Move the globe forward in its orbit a few degrees, and observe that this movement has carried the pointer *L* so many degrees *east* and *north* on the ecliptic, but has *not* changed its *longitude* to so great an amount as would have been the case if *all* the movement had been directly east, or *with the rotation*, instead of being at an angle to it. Bring the calendar index to March 20, rotate the globe until the prime meridian is directly under the pointer *L* ; move the globe forward in the orbit until the pointer L, tracing the ecliptic, is brought to the 10th parallel. Observe that the orbit movement has carried the sun *east* and *north* ; rotate the globe slowly on its axis from west to

*The velocity at which a planet travels depends upon its distance from the sun. The nearer to the sun the greater is his attraction, and the greater the velocity must be to keep the planet from going to him. The orbit of the earth is an ellipse, and the sun is situated in one of the foci. In obedience to this law the earth travels faster when near perihelion (Dec , Jan., Feb.,) than when near aphelion (June, July, Aug.) Other things being equal, it follows that the solar days are longer in Winter than in Summer.

east, and observe this movement carries the pointer *L* back to the prime meridian not on the line of the *ecliptic*, but following the *parallel*. Thus the orbital movement carries the sun forward on an angle, and the daily rotation brings it back on a straight line describing two lines of a triangle, of which the ecliptic is the hypothenuse, a parallel of latitude and the prime meridian being the other two sides.

Owing to the angling movement about 1-12 of the displacement is *lost*, thereby shortening the solar day 1-12 of 3 minutes 56 seconds (the average displacement), or about 20 seconds. *b.* Move the globe forward to the position it occupies about the 1st of June, and observe that from this time until about August 1st the movement of the sun on the ecliptic is *nearer* in the direction of the rotation than in March. Also, that a degree on the *ecliptic* is greater than a degree upon the parallels to which the sun is, at this season, vertical, and the daily rotation is slower.* Owing to this, about 1-12 of this displacement is *gained*, thereby lengthening the solar day 1-12 of 3 minutes 56 seconds, or about 20 seconds.

The Tides.

The Subjoined Explanation of the Mathematics of the Tidal Movements is by Prof. E. Colbert, the well known Astronomer of the Chicago Tribune.

The waters of the ocean are in ceaseless motion, rising and falling twice in each lunar day, or about every 25

---

*The surface of the earth at the equator travels faster in its diurnal motion than the surface at the the tropics, being nearly 250 miles *farther* from the earth's axis.

hours. The rising of the waters is called the *flow* or
flood tide, and the falling of the same the *ebb tide*. The
height to which the waters rise through a number of
succeeding tides is not uniform, as will be explained hereafter. The greater are called Spring, and the lesser
Neap tides. The waters act in obedience to that one
universal law of gravity, which may be expressed as
follows ;   .

*All bodies attract all other bodies throughout space
directly in proportion to the quantity of matter they contain, and inversely as the squares of the distance be-.
tween them.* We may further add that the force of attraction is exerted in the direction of a straight line joining their centers of gravity. The subjoined example
will explain the application of this law.

Let two bodies be placed ten feet apart, the weight of
A to be 2 tons and that of B 1 ton ; their attraction for
each other is directly as their matter, or as 2 is to 1.

Let 10 equal the *power* of attraction of A for B and
5 equal the *power* of attraction of B for A. Separate
the bodies 20 feet ; they now attract each other in the
same ratio, *i. e.* 2 to 1, but with diminished *power*. The
square of the first distance (10 feet) is $10 \times 10 = 100$.
The square of the second distance (20 feet) is 20×20
$= 400$. According to the law above given the attracting power of A and B in the two positions is *inversely*,
as 100 is to 400, or *directly*, as 400 is to 100, or as 4 to 1
in the respective distances of 10 and 20 feet. Thus we
see that at 10 feet the attractive power is four times
greater than it is at 20 feet. If, as stated, the attracting
power of A for B at 10 feet is 2, at 20 feet it is $2 \div 4$

$= \frac{2}{4}$ or $\frac{1}{2}$. For B at 10 feet the power is 1, at 20 feet it is $1 \div 4 = \frac{1}{4}$.

The average tide producing influence of the moon as compared with that of the sun is nearly as $2\frac{1}{2}$ is to 1. The tides in open ocean do not rise to exceed $5\frac{7}{8}$ feet, while in the breakers of the tidal wave as it reaches a continent the water rises very much higher. In the Bay of Fundy, the waters sometimes rise nearly 100 feet. At Boston the tide is usually about 14 feet.

The tides of our oceans are due to the *difference* between the attractive force exerted by the moon and sun ; on the earth as a whole, and on the waters at her surface. The following explanation of the theory of the tides only applies strictly to such parts of the ocean surface as are not near to considerable masses of land surface. The retardation of the tidal wave in moving through shallow water, with the changes in its direction, speed, and volume, caused by continents and islands, are matters which belong more to physical geography than to astronomy. It may be well to note, however, that even in the deep waters of the mid Pacific, the tidal wave is retarded by the same cause that makes it travel behind the moon instead of keeping directly under her ;—friction. The tide wave that gathers on the eastern side of the Pacific Ocean follows about two hours behind the moon, and occupies about 40 hours in passing round to our Atlantic coast ;—less than a cercumference of the globe.

Let M represent the position of the moon ; A D the earth, and E its center. If we take E A, or E D, the

earth's radius, as unity, then, for the least possible distance of the moon; $MA = 55$; $ME = 56$; and MD
$= 57$ nearly.

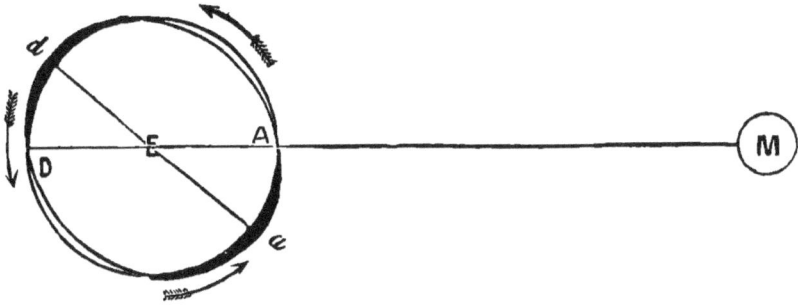

Let m denote the measure of the moon's attractive
force at the unit of distance; it equals about 375,800
feet. Then the disturbing force on the water at A will
be measured by

$$\frac{m}{(55)^2} - \frac{m}{(56)^2} ;= \quad 4.40 \text{ feet.}$$

Similarly; the moon's disturbing force on the water
at D is measured by:

$$\frac{m}{(56)^2} - \frac{m}{(57)^2} ; = \quad 4\cdot17 \text{ feet.}$$

We may also calculate that $\frac{2\,m}{(56)^3} = 4\cdot28$; which is
the mean of the above results, and is the mean tide due
to the moon acting at her least possible distance. The
calculation gives $0\cdot12$ more for the tide under the moon,
and $0\cdot11$ less for the opposite tide. The differences are
really much less than this; owing to the fact that the
crests of the two tides are at a and d instead of on the
line AD. In the open ocean they lag about 43 degrees
behind the place of the moon, and its opposite; and are
still more retarded when they meet with land masses.

The greatest possible distance of the moon from the earth's center is about 64 times the earth's equatorial radius. Calculating as before, we have :

Direct tide $= \dfrac{m}{(63)^2} - \dfrac{m}{(64)^2}$; $=$ 2·94 feet.

Opposite tide $= \dfrac{m}{(64)^2} - \dfrac{m}{(65)^2}$; $=$ 2·80 feet.

Mean tide $= \dfrac{2\,m}{(64)^3}$; $=$ 2·87 feet.

In this case, as in the other, the tide equals $2m$ divided by the cube of the relative distance from the earth's center, plus and minus a small quantity. All perturbations due to the force of attraction vary inversely as the cube of the relative distance, plus or minus a correction which decreases with an increase in the relative distance.

The least and greatest distances of the moon in her (average) orbit, are about 57 and 63½. These correspond to 4·06 feet, and 2·94 feet respectively. Half the sum of these two is 3·5 feet, which is about the average height of crest of the lunar tide wave in the open ocean.

The sun also causes a tide. Our distance from him when in Perihelion is 23,020, and when in Aphelion 23,805 times the earth's equatorial radius. The value of m, for these assumptions of distance of the sun, is 8,900,000,000,000, nearly. The resulting values of the solar tide are 1·44 and 1·30 feet ; average 1·37 feet.

The lunar and the solar tides move after the place of their respective causes in the heavens, as the earth turns round under them. At the times of New and Full Moon the two forces coincide, and the united tide is equal in magnitude to the sum of the two : being (4·06 + 1·44) =5·50 feet, when the earth is nearest to sun and moon ; and (2·94 + 1·30) = 4·24 feet, when both are at their greatest distance. When the moon is in her first or third quarters, the depression caused by the sun coincides with the elevation caused by the moon ; and the tide varies from (4·06 — 1·30) = 2·76 feet, when the moon is in perigee and the earth in aphelion, to (2·94 — 1·44) =1·5 feet, when the moon is in apogee and the earth in perihelion.

The crest of each direct tide is theoretically 40 to 45 degrees or about 2 hours 50 minutes, *late* on the parallel of latitude corresponding to the declination of body causing the tide. That is, if the moon be in 20 degrees north declination, the direct lunar tide will be in 20 degrees of north latitude. The crest of the opposite tide is, similarly, moving in latitude opposite to the declination. Let u denote the angular distance of any point on the earth's surface from the crest of the lunar wave at a given moment ; w its angular distance from the crest of the solar wave at the same instant ; A, the height of the lunar crest ; and B, the height of the solar crest. Then the height of the tide at the designated time and place, will equal :

$$A. \cos. (2\ u) + B. \cos. (2\ w) :$$

remembering that the cosine of an angle greater than 90 degrees and less than 270 degrees, is essentially negative.

The Solar System *

THE SOLAR SYSTEM, as known to us through the discoveries of Copernicus, Kepler, Newton, and their successors, consists of the Sun as a central body, around which revolve the major and minor planets with their satellites, a few periodic comets, and an unknown number of meteor swarms.

The bodies of the system may be classified as follows : 1. The SUN, the center of our portion of the universe or the solar system. 2. Four inner planets, *Mercury, Venus, Earth, Mars*. 3. A group of small planets called *Asteroids*, revolving outside of the orbit of Mars. 4. A group of four outer planets, *Jupiter, Saturn, Uranus and Neptune*. 5. The satellites revolving about their primaries, the planets. 6. A number of comets and meteor swarms revolving in very eccentric orbits about the sun. The 8 planets of groups 2 and 4 are called *Major planets*, to distinguish them from the 200 or more *Minor planets* of group 3.

The relative sizes of the planets, if viewed from an equal distance from all of them, would be somewhat as follows : Jupiter, 1⅗ inches in diameter ; Saturn, 1⅛ inches ; Neptune, 9-16 inches ; Uranus, ½ inch ; Earth and Venus, less than ⅓ inch ; Mars a pin-head, and mercury a little more than a point.

The relative sizes of the Sun as seen from the different planets would be somewhat as follows : From Mercury the Sun would appear 1⅗ inches in diameter; from Venus, ¾ inch; from Earth, ½ inch; Mars, ⅜ inch; Jupiter, 1-16 inch; Saturn, 1-20 inch; Uranus, 1-50 inch; Neptune, a mere point.

If we represent the sun by a gilded globe, 2 feet in diameter, we must show Vulcan and Mercury by mustard seeds ; Venus by a pea, Earth by another, Mars by half that size, Asteroids by the motes in a sunbeam, Jupiter by a small orange, Uranus by a cherry, and Neptune by one a little larger.

The relative distances of the planets from the sun may be represented approximately by these figures: Mercury 4, Venus 7, Earth 10, Mars 15, Ceres (a Minor planet) 28, Jupiter 52, Saturn 95, Uranus 192, Neptune 300.

THE SUN.—The distance of the Sun from us is said to be about 92½ million miles. No one could even count this number in a year's time ! The diameter of the Sun is 860,000 miles ; hence his radius is twice the mean distance of the Moon from the Earth. The Sun's volume is 1,300,000 times that of the Earth, and his mass over 700 times that of all the other bodies, including Earth. Hence, the center of gravity of the whole system is very little outside of the body of the Sun, and will be inside of it when Jupiter and Saturn are in the opposite directions. The Earth receives less than one two-billionth part of the solar heat or radiation ! How much heat then is lost in space ! But suppose the source of our heat supply to be gradually diminished for some cause, how fatal the consequence to the inhabitants of Earth ! Among the theories as to the source of heat supply in the Sun is this, viz., that there is a constant contraction of the solar sphere. Theory indicates that in five million years the Sun will be reduced to half its present size. His density is about one-fourth that of the Earth. Zöllner says the Sun revolves on its axis at the rate of 660 miles an hour.

MERCURY.—But little is known of this planet. Being so near the sun it can be seen only just after sunset or before sunrise, and scarcely ever visible without a telescope. Mercury and Venus have much in common, both being within the orbit of the Earth. Mercury is about 36 million miles from the Sun. His diameter is about 3,000 miles. His year is about 88 of our days ; axial revolution about the same as ours; orbital velocity, 1,773 miles a minute.

VENUS.—This is called the second planet, her year being about 225 of our days; distance from Sun, 66,750,000 miles; diameter, 7,660 miles; orbital velocity, 1,300 miles a minute. Venus may be as near Earth as 22,000,000 miles, or as far as 160,000,000.

EARTH.—This is the third planet in distance from the Sun, and moves in her yearly orbit 69,000 miles per hour, 1,152 miles per minute, or 19 miles per second. In our daily revolution, we, of course, move at the rate of about 1,000 miles per hour.

MOON.—Distance from Earth, nearly 240,000 miles. When in *perigee* she is distant 225,000 miles; when in *apogee* more than 251,000 miles; diameter, 2,153 miles, or less than 3-11 of that of Earth. A body weighing on Earth 1,000 pounds would weigh on the Moon 163 lbs., as her density is but about half that of Earth. The Earth being larger than her satellite, we can see more than nalf her surface, say 58-100. The difference in heat on the Moon at noon and midnight is 500 degrees. The Moon gives us only 1-618,000 as much light as the Sun. The sky full of Moons would not give us daylight.

MARS.—The fourth planet of the system has a year of about 687 days; distance from sun, 141 million miles; diameter, 4,211 miles. It has two moons; day about the same as ours; orbital speed, 900 miles per minute.

JUPITER.—The fifth planet has 4 moons; distance, 480 million miles; volume 1-1,000 that of Sun. His days, 9h. 55m. 20s. He has four satellites; diameter, 86,000 miles. His year equals 12 of ours; velocity, 483 miles a minute.

SATURN.—Annual revolution around the Sun 29½ years; distance from Sun, 881 million miles; diameter, 70,500 miles; volume, 700 times that of Earth. Density, less than that of any other heavenly body, or less than water. Day, 10h. 14m. 24s. It is the most remarkable planet on account of its belt and 8 satellites.

URANUS.—Revolves about the Sun in 84 years; diameter, 50,000 kilometres; has two known satellites; is distant from Sun 1,770,000,000 miles. His year is 84 of ours.

NEPTUNE.—Little is known of this planet. His mean distance is nearly 3 billion miles; periodic time, 164 years; has 1 moon; diameter, 55,000 kilometres, or 34-520 miles.

The air roofs us over, and retaining the heat of the Sun, keeps us warm. The Sun's constant force displayed on the earth is equal to 543 trillions of engines of 400 horse power each, working day and night! A man weighing 150 lbs. on earth, weighs 396 on Jupiter.

Earth is 3,236,000 miles nearer to sun in winter than in summer. Hence it is hotter in the summer of the southern hemisphere than in the northern summer.

SPACE has probably no resisting medium; its temperature is about 200 degrees below zero.

LIGHT goes 185,000 miles a second.

The nearest fixed star is 16 billion miles distant, and it takes three years for light to reach us! The highest speed of a rifle ball is 2,000 feet per second.

The diameters of the asteroids are from 20 to 400 miles. Mass of all of them put together less than one-quarter of earth.

Arago thinks there are about 18 million comets traversing our system. They are thought to be fluid or vapor.

STARS.—There are about 5,000 visible in the whole heavens, both north and south. There are 20 of the 1st magnitude, 65 of the 2nd, 200 of the 3rd, 400 of the 4th, 1,100 of the 5th, 3,200 of the 6th. But of the 7th magnitude there are 13,000 stars, the 8th 40,000, the 9th 142,000. In the Milky Way there are 18 million stars, and when we consider that our Sun is one of the stars of the Milky Way, how wonderful the works of creation, and how insignificant relatively is the earth!

If a railway were built to the sun, and trains upon it were run at the rate of thirty miles an hour, day and night without a stop, it would require three hundred and fifty years to make the journey from the earth to the sun.

If an infant had an arm long enough to enable him to touch the sun with his finger, it would be more than 150 years before he knew that he had burned himself. Yet the material of the sun is but one-fourth as heavy as that of the earth. Hence it would require but 325,000 earths like ours to make a body as heavy as the sun. The sun rotates on its axis once in every twenty-five days. Its circumference at its equator is about 2,580,000 miles. Hence at a given point it moves through space at the rate of 103,200 miles per day, 4,300 miles per hour, and one mile and 18-100 of a mile for every second of time. The man who weighs one hundred and fifty pounds here would weigh more than two tons on the sun, and would be crushed to death by his own weight. The sun's surface is 190,000 times as bright as a candle, and forty-six times as bright as the calcium light. The wind at the surface of the sun often blows with a velocity of from one to three hundred miles a second.

The mechanical equivalent of the heat of the sun is about 10,000 horse-power on every square foot of the sun's surface.

---

* These items are compiled from NEWCOMB and other sources, by E. N. ANDREWS.

81

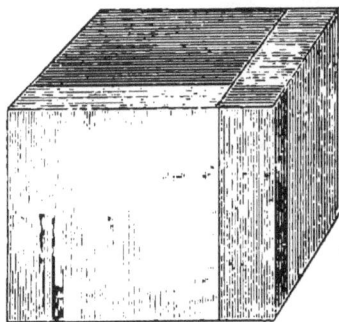

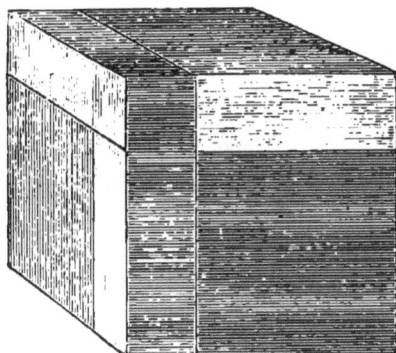

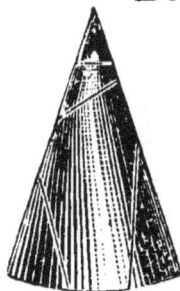

THE "NEW TRIUMPH" SCHOOL DESK.

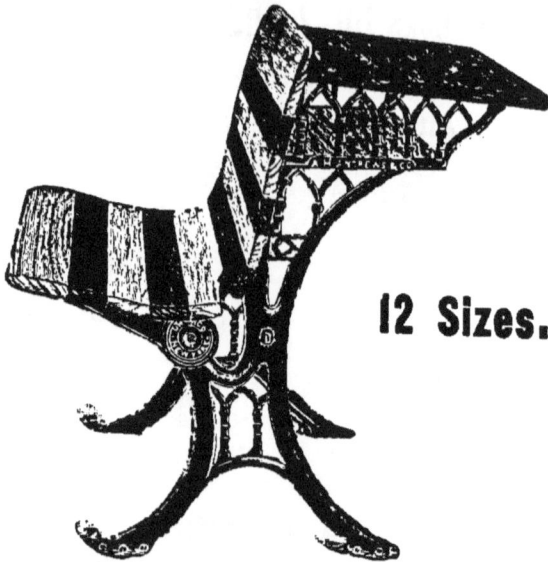

12 Sizes.

UNEQUALED IN
Comfort, Beauty, Strength, and Durability.

A. H. Andrews & Co., Manufacturers,
195 Wabash Avenue, Chicago.

THE NEW FOLDING-LID DESK.

The lid and seat are folding, and reduce the space to a minimum. The lid assumes four positions. Two for study, one for writing, and one as when closed and locked upon the book box.

A. H. Andrews & Co., Manufacturers,
195 Wabash Avenue, Chicago, U. S. A.